AI ESSENTIALS FOR BEGINNERS

LEARN TO USE ARTIFICIAL INTELLIGENCE TO LEVEL UP IN YOUR CAREER, AUTOMATE TASKS, AND MAKE SMARTER DECISIONS– NO TECHNICAL BACKGROUND NEEDED!

KYLE LINDEMANN

CONTENTS

INTRODUCTION

As a millennial approaching middle age, I've had a front-row seat to one of human history's most dramatic technological shifts. If you were born in the 1980s like I was, your world wasn't filled with smartphones, streaming services, or AI-powered assistants—you had corded telephones attached to walls, TVs with only a handful of channels, and if you were lucky, a Nintendo Entertainment System with one controller that barely worked because your best friend smashed the A button too hard while playing Track & Field.

There was no Google, no texting, and no social media—just hand-written notes passed in class and actual conversations with your friends (who had to be physically present because "FaceTime" was just talking to someone in real life). You told your Mom where you would be on a Saturday and then got on your bike to play with your buddies all day before coming home for family dinner without having any idea of anything happening in the outside world.

Then came the Internet Revolution. Suppose you were a teenager in the late '90s. In that case, you remember the excitement of America Online (AOL) and the sound of that iconic dial-up connection—a combination of beeps, screeches, and static that somehow meant you were about to explore a brand-new digital world. Of course, this was also the era when using the internet meant nobody in the house could use the phone. And no, I'm seriously not kidding about that one. Things got so bad in the early days of dial-up that many households had to get a second phone line that was used solely for internet use.

If you were 14 years old and trying to chat with friends on AOL or AIM, nothing was worse than your Mom picking up the landline and instantly ruining your connection. "MOM, GET OFF THE PHONE! I'M TRYING TO DOWNLOAD A PICTURE OF JENNIFER LOVE HEWITT, AND IT'S ONLY 73% LOADED!" Those were dark and painful times.

Fast-forward to adulthood, and everything is digital, wireless, and instant. That same person who grew up rewinding VHS tapes before returning them to Blockbuster now has access to unlimited movies and TV shows at the push of a button. We went from painstakingly burning CDs to curate the perfect mix of songs to now just telling our phones to put on a playlist created by AI based on our current mood. Our workplaces have changed just as drastically—email replaced faxes, Zoom replaced in-person meetings, and AI-powered automation is reshaping how businesses operate. The phrase "Can I speak to a manager?" used to mean a face-to-face confrontation, but now it just means angrily tapping a chatbot until it finally lets you talk to a human.

If you're in your mid-thirties or older, you're part of a unique generation who remembers what life was like before technology took over, yet you've also adapted to every major advancement along the way. You've gone from landlines to iPhones, floppy disks to cloud storage, and waiting 10 minutes for a single webpage to load to getting frustrated if a video buffers for two seconds. It's been a wild ride, and AI is just the latest shift in a lifetime of nonstop technological evolution.

There's a feeling inside us all that often longs for those simpler times when our lives didn't seem so busy, and we weren't bombarded with the 24/7 news cycle or the constant onslaught of social media notifications, but the genie is well out of the bottle now, and there's simply no going back.

If history tells us anything, it's that those who embrace change—not fight it—will thrive in this new digital era.

But what does it all mean? And how do you keep up with all of this new AI technology in a rapidly changing world? Many of you are here because you want to find the right answers while feeling overwhelmed by all the AI that's currently out there, and you're not alone. Even a simple Google search into the world of AI can make you feel like you're trying to drink from a firehouse when all you wanted was just a little sip.

But fear not—I've already done all the legwork to sort through the world of AI to help you digest it all, piece by piece, in a way that's applicable to your own life and makes sense without all the confusing technical jargon.

Imagine you're shopping online for a new pair of shoes. You find a pair you like but decide to hold off on buying them. Later, as you're scrolling through social media, an ad pops up—featuring the same shoes you were looking at from before, along with a discount code. Coincidence? Not at all. That's artificial intelligence (AI) in action, tracking your interests, predicting your next move, and personalizing your experiences without you even realizing it. AI is everywhere, quietly shaping our digital world. This book is your beginner-friendly guide to understanding how it all works—and how it's already influencing your daily life in ways you might not even realize.

Now, what are you thinking: "AI? Isn't that some futuristic technology that only tech geniuses can understand?" Well, I'm here to tell you that's not the case at all! AI is already woven into the fabric of our daily lives, from the personalized recommendations you receive on your favorite streaming platform to the voice assistants that help you manage your schedule. And the best part? You don't need to be a coding whiz or have a Ph.D. in computer science to make the most of this incredible technology.

That's where this book comes in. *AI Essentials for Beginners* is your guide to navigating the exciting world of artificial intelligence, no matter your age or technical background. Whether you're a curious young adult, a professional looking to stay ahead of the curve, or a senior eager to embrace new technologies and not fall behind, this book is for you. We'll unravel the complexities of AI, translating it into easy-to-understand language without all the confusing IT jargon while offering relatable examples that resonate with you.

You might have some reservations about it all. You may have heard rumors that AI is going to steal jobs or that it's only for the tech elite. Let me assure you, those are just myths. AI is here to complement our skills, not replace them. It's a tool that can help you work smarter, not harder, and give you a competitive edge in your career. And the best part? You don't need to be a programming prodigy to reap the benefits.

This book will tackle those burning questions you've always wanted to ask about AI. How does it actually work? How can you apply it to your job or daily life? We'll explore real-world applications, from chatbots that provide instant customer support to algorithms that help doctors diagnose diseases more accurately. You'll discover how AI can help you automate tedious tasks, make better decisions, and even predict future trends.

AI Essentials for Beginners isn't just a dry, technical manual. We'll bring AI to life with engaging stories, some humor, and practical exercises that allow you to experience this technology firsthand. You'll hear from people just like you who have used AI to transform their lives and careers, and you'll gain the confidence to do the same.

As we embark on this journey together, I encourage you to approach AI with a sense of curiosity and an open mind. Don't be intimidated by the jargon or the hype surrounding it all. AI is a tool that's accessible to everyone, and this book will be your trusted companion as you explore its potential. By the end of our time together, you'll have a solid understanding of AI fundamentals, a toolkit of practical applications, and the confidence to use AI to your advantage.

So, whether you're looking to boost your productivity, make well-informed decisions, or simply stay ahead in an ever-changing world, *AI Essentials for Beginners* is your key to unlocking the power of artificial intelligence. Let's dive in and discover how AI can transform your life, one byte at a time! I promise it's a journey that you won't regret.

1

UNDERSTANDING THE BASICS OF ARTIFICIAL INTELLIGENCE

Have you ever wondered why your smartphone seems to know you better than your best friend does? One moment, you're casually searching for cat videos, and the next, your phone is bombarding you with ads for the latest cat toys. It's almost like it's reading your mind, right? But rest assured, it's not telepathy. It's the magic of artificial intelligence quietly working its wonders behind the scenes, making sure your digital life runs smoothly. However, the constant bombardment of advertisements in daily life can be annoying.

In this chapter, we're going to peel back the digital curtain and reveal how AI has subtly integrated itself into your everyday life, often in ways you've never even noticed. We're talking about those little nudges and conveniences that make life just a tad bit easier, like reminding you of an upcoming appointment or suggesting a new show to binge-watch based on your past obsessions. And the best part? No PhD in computer science is required to get the gist of it. Just bring your sense of curiosity and maybe a cup of coffee—AI loves a good caffeinated partner.

You will also be introduced to ChatGPT (one of the best AI tools out there), and at the end of each chapter, I'll provide you with a useful ChatGPT prompt that relates to what you just read so you can start using it right away (if you'd like to, of course). You'll also be given a brief recap at the end of each chapter to help you easily digest what you just learned and how you can apply it to your daily life.

Are you overwhelmed? Don't be. Together, we'll break it all down slowly, piece by piece, to get you as acclimated and comfortable as possible.

1.1 AI IN EVERYDAY LIFE: SURPRISING PLACES YOU ALREADY USE IT

Let's start with those virtual assistants. You know, the ones with the soothing voices that seem to know everything? Siri, Alexa, and Google Assistant are your digital sidekicks, always ready to answer questions, set reminders, and play your favorite tunes. They're not just fun gadgets; they're powered by AI to understand and interpret natural language, making your requests just a voice command away. Whether you're asking Siri to text your friend or telling Alexa to dim the lights, these assistants are designed to improve our lives, even if they might seem confusing or overwhelming at first.

Then there's the mysterious world of personalized recommendations. Have you ever wondered how Netflix always seems to know what you want to watch next? Or how Spotify curates playlists that match your ever-changing moods perfectly? It's not magic; it's an AI that uses algorithms to analyze your viewing and listening habits to predict what you'd enjoy. It's like having your very own entertainment guru, minus the hefty consulting fees. This kind of predictive power is what keeps us glued to our screens, discovering new favorites with little effort on our part.

AI doesn't stop at entertainment, though. It's quietly revolutionizing our homes, too. Take smart thermostats, for example. These nifty gadgets learn your temperature preferences over time, adjusting the climate before you even realize you're too hot or too cold. And let's not forget about AI-powered security cameras that recognize familiar faces, sending you alerts only when something's amiss. It's like having a vigilant guardian, always on duty to keep your home safer. These technologies seamlessly integrate into our routines, making home life more convenient and secure without us even realizing it.

And finally, AI is hitting the road, quite literally, with transportation. GPS and route optimization are the unsung heroes of modern travel, using AI to calculate the quickest routes in real-time, helping you dodge traffic jams and construction delays with ease. But the real showstopper? Autonomous vehicles. These self-driving cars are not just a sci-fi dream anymore; they're a reality that could redefine how we commute. While fully autonomous vehicles are still navigating the regulatory landscape, the prospect of a car that chauffeurs you around while you relax in the back seat is within reach. How's that for a glimpse into the future?

So, as you can see, AI is not just a buzzword. It's a practical, everyday technology that enhances our lives, works, and plays. From virtual assistants to personalized entertainment, smart homes to intelligent navigation, AI is here to stay, and it's only getting smarter. And the best part? You can just sit back, relax, and let AI do all the heavy lifting.

1.2 DISCUSSING THE EVOLUTION OF AI

I'll spare you the long classroom lecture on the history of AI and how it came to be, but let's take a quick trip back in time to when the seeds of AI were first planted—a time when computers were the size of refrigerators, and the internet was just a twinkle in some scientist's eye. Enter Alan Turing, the brilliant mind who, in the 1930s, began pondering the idea of machines that could think. Turing wasn't just a cryptanalyst who helped crack codes during World War II; he pioneered concepts that laid the groundwork for AI. His famous Turing Test, introduced in 1950, was a simple yet profound idea: if a machine could converse with a human indistinguishably from another human, it could be considered intelligent.

Fast-forward a few decades, and the world saw IBM's Deep Blue, a chess-playing computer, defeat world champion Garry Kasparov in 1997—a moment that screamed to the world that AI was no longer just science fiction.

But Turing wasn't alone in his visionary pursuits. John McCarthy, another titan in the field, coined the term "artificial intelligence" in 1956 and helped establish AI as a distinct area of computer science. McCarthy's work emphasized the potential for machines to solve problems and perform tasks that, until then, required human intelligence. Thanks to these pioneers, AI has evolved from a mere concept to a vital technology shaping our daily lives.

Now, let's discuss some of the ways AI impacts us today. Consider search engines, those digital librarians that sift through mountains of data to find exactly what you're looking for. They use AI to understand your queries and provide the most relevant results, saving you from the dreaded rabbit hole of endless links that don't bring you any closer to your goal. And spam filters in your email inbox? They're the unsung heroes, using AI to distinguish between that important email from your boss and another discount offer you never signed up for. AI's ability to sort and prioritize helps keep our communication streamlined and efficient.

Then there's the magic of real-time language translation. Picture this: you're traveling abroad, trying to order a meal, and your language skills are limited to "hello" and "thank you." AI steps in, translating your requests on the fly, bridging cultural gaps, and facilitating communication in ways previously unimagined. This kind of technology fosters global connections, allowing us to interact and understand each other better, no matter where we are. It's like having a personal translator in your pocket, ready to assist instantly.

AI's evolution is not just a story of technological milestones; it's about how these advancements have become integral to our everyday experiences. Whether we're searching, communicating, or traveling, AI quietly enhances our capabilities, making tasks smoother and more intuitive. It's a testament to human ingenuity, bringing abstract concepts to life and embedding them in the fabric of our world.

1.3 WHAT AI REALLY IS: BREAKING DOWN THE FUNDAMENTALS

Picture artificial intelligence as that super smart friend who seems to have a knack for everything—except, in this case, it's a machine. At its core, AI is about mimicking human intelligence processes using computer systems. Imagine a brainy robot that's been taught how to learn, reason, and even correct itself when it makes a mistake. These abilities make AI unique, and this learning process involves algorithms and data, which are the building blocks of AI. Algorithms are like recipes; they provide step-by-step instructions. Data, on the other hand, is the endless pantry of ingredients that AI uses to whip up its solutions. Together, they form the foundation on which AI operates, making it capable of performing tasks with a level of sophistication that makes you wonder if you should start setting a place at the dinner table for your laptop.

Let's clarify how AI stands apart from traditional programming and automation. Traditional programming is all about giving computers a strict set of rules to follow. Think of it like following a GPS: you input a destination, and it tells you exactly which turns to make. AI, however, is more like a seasoned traveler. It doesn't just follow directions; it learns the best routes over time, adapts to detours, and even suggests scenic stops along the way. Automation executes tasks based on pre-defined rules, while AI uses intelligent decision-making to adapt and improve. This adaptability allows AI to learn from data and adjust its actions accordingly, unlike automation, which sticks to its script no matter what.

However, as impressive as AI is, it does have its limitations. While it's great at identifying patterns, like a detective solving a mystery, it lacks the human touch of intuition. AI can recognize trends in data, but understanding important context or the nuances of human emotions remains a challenge. It's like that friend who can tell you the best stock options but can't quite grasp why you're crying during a sappy movie. Despite these limits, AI is brilliant at tasks like pattern recognition and data analysis.

AI is not just a technological marvel; it's a blend of curiosity, innovation, and the quest to understand and replicate the human mind. It's the culmination of years of research, trial and error, and a testament to human ingenuity. As we continue to explore its potential, AI invites us to reimagine what's possible, challenging us to push the boundaries of what machines can achieve.

1.4 DEBUNKING AI MYTHS: SEPARATING FACT FROM FICTION

Let's tackle the elephant in the room—AI taking over all our jobs. Picture this: a world where robots do everything from flipping burgers to writing novels. Sounds like science fiction, right? The reality is far less dramatic. AI is more like that eager office intern who's great at handling repetitive tasks, freeing up humans to do what they do best: think creatively and solve complex problems. While AI can automate certain roles, it also helps to create new opportunities in the process. For example, it can analyze heaps of data faster than any human can, assisting businesses in making well-informed decisions. But the good news is that jobs requiring empathy, strategy, and human interaction are here to stay. So, rather than fearing a robot uprising, we should focus on how AI can enhance our work, making us more productive and innovative in our daily lives.

Now, the notion of AI consciousness is another fascinating myth. We've all seen movies like Terminator, where machines gain self-awareness and plot against their creators. Fortunately, that remains purely fictional. AI lacks consciousness, emotions, or desires. It doesn't daydream about world domination or harbor grudges. AI systems follow algorithms without understanding the content. They process data and churn out results but don't "think" or "feel" in any human sense. So, unless you're a toaster with aspirations of grandeur, you're in the clear. AI remains a tool—a remarkably sophisticated one—but still a tool that requires human oversight to guide its use and mitigate risks.

AI has its limits, too. It excels at processing information but falls short in understanding emotions or context. That's AI and human emotions in a nutshell. While AI can analyze sentiment in text, it doesn't genuinely "get" emotions. That's where we, the humans, come in. Our ability to empathize and interpret context remains unmatched. So, as AI evolves, our role is to guide and oversee its use, ensuring it serves humanity's best interests. AI is a powerful ally, but like any tool, it requires a human touch to steer its course effectively.

1.5 MACHINE LEARNING VS. DEEP LEARNING: A SIMPLE COMPARISON

Machine learning and deep learning are two important branches of artificial intelligence (AI) that help computers learn from data and make decisions without being specifically programmed to do so. Think of machine learning as teaching a computer to recognize patterns—like how a music app learns your favorite songs and suggests new ones based on your listening habits. Deep learning takes this a step further by using complex networks that attempt to mimic how the human brain processes information. Deep learning allows AI to tackle more advanced tasks, like recognizing faces in photos or translating languages in real-time. Both are essential in making AI smarter and more capable, powering everything from virtual assistants to self-driving cars.

Both machine learning and deep learning are transforming industries in different ways. Machine learning is great for analyzing numbers and predicting trends, helping businesses forecast sales or detect fraud. On the other hand, deep learning is a powerhouse for visual and speech recognition, making it essential in detecting diseases from medical scans in the healthcare field. Think of machine learning as innovative research, sorting through past information to make educated guesses, while deep learning is the creative problem solver, uncovering hidden details we might miss. Together, they are shaping the future of AI and innovation.

1.6 BEGINNERS GUIDE TO CHATGPT

If you've ever wished for a personal assistant who could help answer questions, spark ideas, and even write things for you, then ChatGPT is exactly that—an AI-powered chatbot designed to assist you in a conversation-like way. It's like having a super-smart friend who can talk to you, help with emails, brainstorm creative ideas, and even explain complex topics in simple terms. Unlike traditional search engines that just provide links to websites, ChatGPT generates direct, human-like responses, making it feel more like a real conversation rather than just looking up information.

Using ChatGPT is as easy as typing a message. You start by entering a prompt, which is simply a question or a request, and ChatGPT will respond instantly. You can ask it to write, explain, summarize, suggest ideas, or even have a casual conversation. Whether you need help crafting a professional email, learning a new skill, or coming up with a fun social media caption, all you have to do is tell ChatGPT what you need, and it will generate a response in seconds. The more specific and detailed your prompt is, the better and more accurate the answer will be.

ChatGPT has tons of useful features that make it a powerful tool. It can assist with writing tasks like drafting articles, social media posts, and resumes. It can help with learning by breaking down complicated topics into simpler explanations, making it great for students or anyone looking to understand something brand-new. Furthermore, it can generate ideas for businesses, projects, or creative writing. ChatGPT can be your go-to AI companion if you're stuck on a problem, need inspiration, or want to chat.

The best part? ChatGPT keeps learning and improving. While it doesn't have real-time internet access, it has been trained on vast knowledge and can provide helpful insights on a wide range of topics. It's always available—24/7—and can be used on different devices, making it a convenient tool for work, learning, or everyday tasks. The more you use it, the better you'll get at crafting prompts that give you the best responses. Whether you're here to boost productivity, learn something new, or have fun experimenting with AI, ChatGPT is a game-changer that makes interacting with technology easier than ever.

Getting Setup with ChatGPT

Now, let's get you set up with ChatGPT so you can start enjoying its capabilities. Step one: account creation. This is as easy as creating an account on your favorite social media platform—no need to crack codes or solve puzzles. Visit the ChatGPT website (https://openai.com/chatgpt/overview/), click on the 'Sign Up' button, and follow the prompts.

Once you've started your account, it's time for the initial setup. Here, you'll want to configure settings and preferences to tailor ChatGPT to your needs. Think of it as customizing your coffee order—do you want it to focus on certain topics or keep responses brief and to the point? As you learn how to use ChatGPT, you can adjust these settings to get the best user experience.

Of course, even the best technology can have its hiccups. You might encounter a rare response error where ChatGPT doesn't quite hit the mark in its replies. Don't panic; it happens to the best of us. If a response seems off, consider rephrasing your question or providing more context to guide it. Connectivity issues can also rear their head, especially if your internet connection is playing hide and seek. Ensure you're connected to a stable network to prevent interruptions. It's the digital equivalent of ensuring you're speaking into the right end of the phone.

ChatGPT can be your ultimate tool for productivity, creativity, and education. It's a versatile assistant ready to help tackle tasks, brainstorm ideas, or simply have an interesting conversation.

Mastering Prompts: How to Get the Best Responses from ChatGPT

Using ChatGPT is simple, but knowing how to craft and refine your prompts can make all the difference. Think of prompts as instructions—you tell ChatGPT what you need, and it does its best to deliver. A little strategy goes a long way in getting clear, helpful, and tailored responses to your needs. Here's how to do it:

1. Copy the Prompt or Write Your Own

If you find a ready-made prompt that fits your task, copy it exactly as it's written. If you're creating your own, keep it clear and direct. The more specific you are, the better ChatGPT will understand what it is you are asking.

2. Paste It Into ChatGPT and Press Enter

Open ChatGPT, paste your prompt into the message box and hit enter. It's that easy! ChatGPT will process your request and generate a response based on what you asked.

3. Customize and Refine for Better Results

If the response isn't quite what you wanted, don't worry—adjusting the prompt can improve it. Try adding more details, such as a specific tone, format, or topic. For example, instead of saying, *"Write an email,"* you could say, *"Write a professional email to a client, thanking them for their business and offering a discount on their next purchase."* The more context you give ChatGPT, the more accurate and helpful the response will be.

4. Review, Adjust, and Experiment

ChatGPT is smart, but sometimes you'll need to tweak things to get the best answer. If the response isn't quite right, reword your prompt or ask ChatGPT to refine its answer. Experimenting with different phrasings and levels of detail can unlock even better results. Over time, you'll get a feel for what works best, making ChatGPT an even more powerful tool for you.

Key Takeaways on the Benefits of Using ChatGPT:

- **Instant Answers & Research Support**—Instead of sifting through endless Google results, ChatGPT can summarize complex topics, explain difficult concepts, and provide quick answers with easy-to-understand explanations. ChatGPT can streamline the research process if you need a quick history lesson, help to understand a financial term, or assistance with a work project.
- **Boosting Creativity & Brainstorming**—Are you struggling with writer's block? Do you need fresh marketing ideas for your business? Do you want to come up with the perfect caption for social media? ChatGPT can generate creative ideas, refine your writing, and help you brainstorm solutions, whether you're working on a blog post, script, or business plan.

- **Learning & Skill Development** – You can use ChatGPT as a personalized tutor to learn a new language, improve your resume, prepare for an interview, or even gain insights into coding, finance, or design. It's a powerful tool to help you level up your knowledge and stay ahead in your career without needing to sign up for expensive courses.
- **Time-Saving & Task Automation** – ChatGPT can help draft emails, reports, schedules, and summaries in seconds. Instead of spending hours crafting the perfect message or figuring out how to phrase something professionally, you can let AI do the heavy lifting while you focus on more important tasks.
- **Every Day Problem-Solving & Advice** – Need meal planning ideas, fitness recommendations, or travel tips? ChatGPT can provide insights, suggestions, and customized advice to make daily decision-making easier. Whether it's finding a great gift or deciding how to fix a home repair issue, ChatGPT is like having an on-demand personal assistant for everyday life.

ChatGPT isn't just for tech experts or businesses—it's an AI-powered tool designed to help anyone save time, boost creativity, and improve productivity. Whether you're using it for work, personal projects, or everyday problem-solving, it's a valuable resource as powerful as you make it.

1.7 A JARGON-FREE GLOSSARY OF BASIC AI TERMS

Jumping into AI might feel like learning a new language, but don't worry—I've got you covered. Let's start with the basics. An algorithm is just a fancy way of saying "a set of instructions." Think of it like a recipe—it tells the computer exactly what steps to take to solve a problem.

Even in the sports world, NFL teams are no longer just relying on gut instincts and highlight reels to find their next superstar—they're leaning heavily on algorithms to predict which rookies in the NFL Draft will thrive at the next level. These advanced models crunch mountains of data, analyzing everything from college production, athletic testing, and injury history to more nuanced factors like play speed tracked by GPS, route efficiency, and how a player performs in high-pressure situations. A well-crafted algorithm can pinpoint hidden gems by identifying patterns that traditional scouting might miss—like a wide receiver who consistently separates against press coverage but lacks elite top-end speed, or a linebacker whose reaction time and tackling efficiency suggest he'll excel despite an average forty-yard dash time. The best part? These algorithms continuously refine themselves, learning from past draft successes and failures, helping teams minimize risk and maximize value when they're on the clock.

AI is powered by big data, which is what it sounds like—a massive collection of information that helps AI systems learn and make smarter decisions. But where does all that data get processed? That's where cloud computing comes in. Instead of needing a supercomputer on your desk, cloud computing lets AI tools run on powerful servers over the internet, making AI accessible to everyone. These aren't just buzzwords—they're the building blocks of AI, shaping how we work, communicate, and interact with technology daily.

Now, you didn't come here to be bombarded with AI-related lingo. You're here because you want to know more about AI and how to use it in ways that apply to your own life, and I promise you we'll be getting to that very soon.

As we wrap up this chapter, remember that these terms are the foundation to unlock the potential of AI in our everyday lives. With this newfound understanding, you're better equipped to navigate the discussions and innovations in AI, making even the most complex concepts feel a little more manageable. Who knew a few words could open so many doors?

AI is not just a buzzword—it's an integral part of the modern world, and it's only going to get smarter. Whether for work, entertainment, or everyday convenience, AI is here to enhance our lives, not replace them. Now that you've got a solid foundation in what AI is and how it works, it's time to dive deeper into how it's reshaping industries, businesses, and even our own career opportunities in the chapters ahead.

Glossary of Basic AI Terms for Your Reference

- **Algorithm** – A step-by-step set of instructions that tells a computer exactly what to do to solve a problem or complete a task. Think of it like a recipe for a dish—each step is carefully laid out so that the final product turns out right.
- **Artificial Intelligence (AI)** – The ability of a computer or machine to mimic human intelligence by learning, reasoning, problem-solving, and even recognizing speech or images. If you've ever asked Alexa or Siri a question, you've already interacted with AI!
- **Automation** – The use of AI to perform tasks without human involvement, ranging from chatbots handling customer service to robots assembling factory products.
- **Big Data** – A massive collection of information that is too large for traditional computers to process. AI helps make sense of big data by organizing it, finding patterns, and turning it into useful insights—think of how Netflix recommends shows based on what you've watched.
- **Chatbot** – A computer program that simulates a conversation with a human. Chatbots use AI to answer questions, provide customer support, or even tell jokes (although their humor can still be hit or miss).

- **ChatGPT** - An AI-powered chatbot that understands and responds to text like a human in a conversation. It can help answer questions, generate ideas, write content, summarize information, and assist with learning or work-related tasks. You interact with ChatGPT by typing a question or request (called a prompt), and it provides a response in seconds. It's like having a virtual assistant that's available 24/7 to help with writing, brainstorming, problem-solving, and more.
- **Cloud Computing** – The process of storing and accessing data or software over the internet instead of on your personal computer. This is what allows you to stream movies on Netflix, store files in Google Drive, or use AI-powered apps without downloading anything.
- **Computer Vision** – A form of AI that enables computers to "see" and understand images or videos. This technology is used in facial recognition, self-driving cars, and medical imaging.
- **Data Mining** – The process of digging through large amounts of data to find patterns, trends, or useful information. Businesses constantly use this to predict what customers want, like when Amazon suggests products based on what you've browsed.
- **Deep Learning** – A specialized type of machine learning that teaches computers to recognize patterns using multiple layers of information—kind of like how a brain works. This is what powers facial recognition on smartphones and how AI can identify objects in photos.
- **Explainable AI (XAI)** – AI systems that are designed to explain how they make decisions, so humans can understand and trust them. It's the difference between AI saying, "Because I said so," and actually showing the work it did.
- **Generative AI** – A type of AI that creates new content, like text, images, music, or videos, based on what it has learned

from existing data. This is the technology behind AI art generators and chatbots like ChatGPT.

- **Machine Learning (ML)** – A type of AI where computers learn from experience without being directly programmed. The more data they process, the smarter they get—just like how Spotify learns your music taste and suggests new songs.
- **Natural Language Processing (NLP)** – The ability of AI to understand and interact with human language, whether spoken or written. This is what allows AI assistants like Siri or ChatGPT to understand and respond to your questions.
- **Neural Network** – A system designed to function like a human brain, using layers of artificial "neurons" that process information and make decisions. This is what helps AI recognize speech, predict stock market trends, and even generate human-like text in tools like ChatGPT.
- **Predictive Analytics** – AI that uses past data to predict future outcomes. Businesses use it to forecast sales, healthcare providers to predict patient risks, and even Netflix to recommend what you should binge-watch next.
- **Prompt** - the starting point of a conversation with AI. A prompt is the question, instruction, or request you give an AI system to generate a response. Think of it like giving directions to a GPS: the clearer and more specific you are, the better the AI can guide you to the right answer.
- **Reinforcement Learning** – A type of machine learning where an AI learns by trial and error, getting rewarded for good actions and penalized for bad ones. It's similar to training a pet, except AI doesn't need treats—just better data.
- **Supervised Learning** – A type of machine learning where AI is trained using labeled data, meaning it already knows the correct answers and needs to learn how to find them independently.

- **Turing Test** – A test created by Alan Turing to see if a machine can behave so much like a human that people can't tell the difference. If AI can pass this test, it means it has reached a high level of human-like intelligence.
- **Unsupervised Learning** – Unlike supervised learning, this type of AI is given data without labels and has to figure out patterns on its own. It's like giving someone a puzzle without showing them the final picture and asking them to solve it.

Key Takeaways from Chapter 1

- **AI is everywhere, even when we don't realize it.** Whether helping you navigate traffic with GPS, curate the perfect playlist, filter spam emails, or suggest your next bingeworthy show, AI has become an invisible yet indispensable assistant in our daily routines.
- **The evolution of AI started long before today's technology boom.** From Alan Turing's groundbreaking ideas to IBM's Deep Blue defeating a world chess champion, AI has been decades in the making. What was once just a theory has become a reality, shaping how we work, communicate, and drive.
- **AI isn't magic—it's built on data and algorithms.** At its core, AI is about recognizing patterns, learning from experience, and improving over time. Whether it's a recommendation system figuring out your taste in movies or a self-driving car adapting to real-world conditions, AI thrives on data and thoughtful decision-making.
- **Despite its power, AI has limitations.** While it can process vast amounts of information and identify patterns faster than any human, it still lacks intuition, emotional intelligence, and the ability to truly understand context the

way we do. It's a tool—a very advanced one—but still just a tool that requires human oversight.

2
ADDRESSING COMMON MISCONCEPTIONS WITH AI

This chapter is about banishing the myth that AI is a high-tech fortress only accessible to those who can code in their sleep. In reality, AI is more like a buffet—open to everyone, with plenty of options to suit your taste, even if you can't tell an algorithm from an avocado. The good news is if you have a smartphone, a voice assistant, or even an internet connection, you're already halfway there.

Online learning platforms are also stepping up to the plate to break down AI barriers, offering courses that cater to all skill levels. There are beginner's courses available on DeepLearning.AI, which are designed to break down complex concepts into digestible chunks, explaining everything from the basics of machine learning to the intricacies of data science. The best part? You can learn at your own pace, whether that's on a leisurely Sunday afternoon or during your lunch break.

The good news is that the majority of AI applications are designed with the average user in mind. Take voice-command features, for instance. Whether you're asking your phone to play your favorite song or instructing your smart speaker to dim the lights, these interfaces are designed to be as user-friendly as possible. It's like having a personal assistant who never forgets your coffee order or turns off the lights when you leave the room, something that Dads everywhere can celebrate.

And let's not forget the everyday heroes who are using AI without a technical background. Small business owners are leveraging AI to gain insights into customer preferences, improving their services without needing a tech team on standby. Educators are incorporating AI tools to create interactive learning experiences that engage students in new and exciting ways. These individuals are proof that you don't need to be a programmer to benefit from AI—you just need a willingness to explore and experiment.

The democratization of AI education is a movement that's gaining momentum, making AI accessible to everyone, not just the tech elite. Initiatives are popping up worldwide, aiming to broaden the reach of AI knowledge and skills. Programs are being developed to teach AI basics to students, professionals, and anyone with a curious mind. These initiatives are designed to equip people with the tools they need to understand and use AI, opening doors to new opportunities and innovations.

Reflection Exercise: Consider Your AI Comfort Zone

Take a moment to think about how you interact with AI in your daily life. Are there areas where you feel comfortable, like using voice assistants or recommendation systems? What about areas where you feel less confident? Reflect on how you can explore these areas further. Just like with any new endeavor, the goal is not to become an expert overnight but to expand your understanding of AI and its potential applications in your life.

By breaking down the barriers to AI education and use, we're opening the door to a future where AI is a tool for everyone. Whether you're looking to enhance your career, streamline your daily tasks, or simply satisfy your curiosity, AI offers endless possibilities. The key is to approach it with an open mind and a willingness to learn.

2.1 THE ARTIFICIAL INTELLIGENCE BOOM: JUST A FAD OR HERE TO STAY?

Some skeptics have dismissed AI as just another tech trend, a flashy innovation destined to fade like so many before it. But the reality tells a different story. The AI boom isn't just a temporary surge of excitement—it's a full-fledged technological revolution reshaping industries, redefining workflows, and changing the way we interact with the world. From healthcare and finance to marketing and logistics, companies are pouring billions into AI-driven solutions, and the results speak for themselves. AI is streamlining operations, cutting costs, and unlocking possibilities that were unthinkable just a few years ago.

And it's not just businesses that are feeling the impact. AI has quietly woven itself into daily life, becoming a fixture in how people shop, communicate, and manage their time. AI-powered translation apps are breaking down language barriers, and personal finance tools use AI to optimize budgets and savings plans. Whether we realize it or not, AI has become a co-pilot in our decision-making, making everything from work commutes to grocery shopping more efficient.

With AI adoption accelerating in nearly every industry, it's clear this technology isn't going anywhere. The question isn't whether AI will stick around—it's how quickly individuals and businesses can adapt and harness it to their advantage. As with any disruptive innovation, those who embrace AI early will gain the most, positioning themselves ahead of the curve in an era of automation, efficiency, and intelligent computing.

So, instead of wondering if AI will last, the real conversation should be about how we prepare for a future where AI is an ever-present force in both personal and professional settings. Staying ahead means learning, experimenting, and integrating AI into daily workflows. Whether it's improving productivity, enhancing customer experiences, or simply making life more convenient, AI isn't just a tool—it's becoming a necessity, regardless of your age, profession, or where you live.

2.2 AI FOR ALL AGES: IT'S NEVER TOO LATE TO START

You know what they say: age is just a number. This is especially true when it comes to learning about artificial intelligence. Whether you're a teenager, a young adult, a seasoned professional, or someone who's been around the block a few times, AI is as accessible as your morning crossword puzzle. Lifelong learning isn't just a catchy buzzword—it's a reality, and AI is the perfect field to dive into, regardless of the number of birthday candles on your last cake.

Adult learning programs are popping up everywhere, focusing on technology skills that can keep you sharp and adaptable. And for the seniors among us, there are AI courses available on websites like AIandYou, which are crafted with simplified content, proving that you can teach an old dog new tricks—especially when the tricks involve digital assistants and smart gadgets. For the purposes of organization and book flow, links to resources like AIandYou will be provided at the end of your reading.

Intergenerational learning is another exciting frontier, and schools are catching on, too, encouraging students to collaborate with older generations. This not only bridges the age gap but also brings a delightful mix of experience and fresh perspectives. Youngsters can teach the elders how to set up their smart home devices, while the elders can share their wisdom on, say, surviving without Wi-Fi. This shared learning enriches both sides, creating a community where knowledge flows across generations like a well-oiled machine.

Let's talk about AI applications that cater to different age groups. For our seniors, AI health monitoring apps like Medisafe and FollowMy-

Health are like having a mini medical team at home. These apps track vital signs and even remind you to take your meds, ensuring you stay at your healthiest. It's like having a doctor who doesn't mind being on call 24/7. Meanwhile, educational AI games like Machine Learning for Kids are engaging young minds, teaching everything from math to coding in ways that feel more like play than study. These games are designed to adapt to each child's learning pace, making education a personalized and fun-filled adventure. AI's versatility means there's something for everyone, whether you're counting steps or counting sheep.

Of course, diving into AI isn't always a walk in the park, especially for older learners. But fear not! Many AI applications come with simplified user interfaces designed to be as intuitive as possible. Think of them as the IKEA of tech—assembly required, but with clear instructions and maybe a few extra screws. Plus, there are support networks specifically for seniors learning new technologies. These communities provide assistance, answer questions, and create a space where no inquiry is too small or too silly. Whether online forums or local meetups, these networks ensure that everyone has a companion on their tech-learning journey.

So, whether you're eight or eighty, AI has something for you. It's not just about keeping up with technology; it's about embracing it, letting it enhance your life, and having a bit of fun along the way. Learning AI can be as rewarding as a good book or a new hobby, adding another feather to your cap. So go ahead, take the plunge into AI—your future self will thank you.

2.3 AI AND JOB SECURITY: NAVIGATING THE NEW LANDSCAPE

Picture this: you're at your office, sipping your third cup of coffee for the day, and your boss announces an exciting new AI initiative. Suddenly, you find yourself wondering if your job is about to be replaced by a robot that can do everything you do, but with fewer coffee and bathroom breaks. The fear of AI-induced job displacement is a common concern, yet not entirely accurate. While AI is indeed reshaping the job market, it's not the villain in this story. Instead, think of AI as the sidekick that takes over mundane, repetitive tasks, freeing you up to focus on more meaningful work. Automation is here to handle those tedious data entry chores, leaving you with the time and energy to tackle creative projects that require a human touch. So rather than facing redundancy, many workers are finding themselves in new roles that AI has helped create, demanding fresh skills and expertise that are anything but robotic.

This evolving landscape calls for adaptability and the willingness to learn new things. As AI continues to spread its wings, it opens up exciting career transition opportunities. Reskilling programs are popping up like mushrooms after a rainstorm, offering courses focused on equipping workers with AI and digital skills. Platforms like Coursera and Udacity are offering a smorgasbord of online courses on emerging technologies that come with real certifications that you can list on your resume after completing them, ensuring you're not left in the dust. It's a bit like going back to school, but this time, you get to wear your pajamas and avoid the cafeteria food.

Industries across the board are thriving with the integration of AI, transforming how businesses operate and paving the way for improved services. In healthcare, professionals are utilizing AI to enhance patient care, from predictive diagnostics to personalized treatment plans. Imagine a world where doctors can diagnose diseases with pinpoint accuracy, thanks to AI analyzing medical images faster than you can say "x-ray." Meanwhile, financial analysts are leveraging AI for data-driven insights, enabling them to make informed decisions that would make even the savviest Wall Street trader proud. AI's ability to process vast amounts of data in the blink of an eye is revolutionizing industries, allowing them to operate more efficiently and effectively.

Adaptability is the name of the game in today's ever-changing job market. Embracing a growth mindset is crucial, as it allows you to view technological change not as a threat, but as an opportunity to grow and evolve. Being open to learning new skills and exploring different career paths is key to staying relevant and competitive. Networking and professional development in AI-focused fields can be your secret weapon, helping you build connections and gain insights into the latest trends and innovations. By attending conferences, joining AI interest groups, or simply striking up conversations with colleagues, you can stay ahead of the curve and remain a valuable player in your industry.

So, while AI might seem like a daunting force poised to disrupt the world of work, it's also an ally offering opportunities for growth and innovation. By embracing the changes that AI brings, you can navigate this new landscape with confidence, equipped with the skills and knowledge needed to thrive in an AI-enhanced world.

2.4 ADDRESSING ETHICAL CONCERNS: TRUSTING AI APPLICATIONS

Imagine you're setting your fantasy football lineup, and your app's AI-powered projections tell you to bench your star wide receiver for some guy you've barely heard of. You hesitate—because trusting AI feels a lot like trusting that fantasy "expert" who swore a backup tight end with zero catches would go off last week. This is the challenge with AI in real life, too. As it becomes more embedded in our decision-making, transparency is everything. Explainable AI is like breaking down why your fantasy app made that wild recommendation—it shows you the data behind the decision rather than just throwing out a number. Just like you'd want to see a player's target share, red-zone usage, and defensive matchups before trusting the advice, AI users need clarity on how algorithms reach their conclusions. That's why companies are now offering transparency reports, like a scouting breakdown of an NFL prospect, to help users understand what's really happening under the hood. Whether it's AI or fantasy football, blind trust in the system can leave you making the wrong call at the worst possible time.

Ethical AI committees are popping up in organizations, focusing on responsible development and deployment of AI technologies. These committees are like the wise old owls of the tech world, guiding AI systems to adhere to ethical practices and avoid causing harm. By implementing these guidelines, companies can develop AI that benefits society as a whole, ensuring that nobody feels like they got a bad deal with their slice of the digital pie.

Trust is the name of the game when it comes to AI adoption. For users to embrace AI, they need to believe in its reliability and consistency. It's like a good friendship—built on trust and mutual respect. AI systems must perform consistently, providing users with the confidence to rely on them for important tasks. User feedback mechanisms are essential for continuous improvement, acting as a suggestion box where users can voice their concerns and experiences. This feedback helps developers refine AI systems, making them more effective and trustworthy.

The journey of AI from a niche technology to an everyday tool is intertwined with ethical considerations. Just as you wouldn't serve a dish without ensuring it is safe and tasty, AI systems need to be developed with care and responsibility. By focusing on transparency, fairness, and trust, we can create an AI landscape where everyone feels confident and secure. In the next chapter, we'll explore the everyday applications of AI, diving into the myriad ways it's enhancing our lives and simplifying tasks. But for now, let's savor the progress we've made in making AI a trustworthy ally.

Key Takeaways from Chapter 2

- **AI is already a part of your daily life.** If you've ever used a voice assistant, received personalized recommendations on

Netflix, or relied on Google Maps to avoid traffic, congratulations—you've interacted with AI. The technology is quietly making tasks more efficient, whether in entertainment, navigation, or home automation. You don't need to understand the technical details to benefit from it.

- **AI education is more accessible than ever.** Free and affordable online courses from platforms like Coursera, Udacity, and DeepLearning.AI are making it easy for anyone to learn about AI. Whether you want a basic understanding or a deep dive into machine learning, there are resources available for all skill levels. Learning AI isn't about becoming an expert overnight—it's about staying informed and adaptable.
- **AI is for all ages.** It's never too late to start learning about AI. Older generations are using AI for health monitoring and home automation, while younger generations are using it to enhance learning and creativity. The technology is designed to be intuitive, and support networks exist to help people of all ages become comfortable with it.
- **AI is not just for coders and engineers.** You don't need to be a tech expert to use AI. With drag-and-drop platforms like Runway ML and Teachable Machine, even those with zero programming knowledge can harness AI for creative and business purposes. In the same way smartphones once made digital communication effortless, AI is simplifying automation, predictions, and decision-making for everyday users.
- **AI isn't replacing all jobs—it's transforming them.** While AI is automating repetitive tasks, it's also creating new career opportunities. Workers who embrace AI tools can increase their productivity and focus on higher-value tasks that require human creativity and problem-solving. Instead of fearing AI, professionals should look at it as a way

to enhance their skills and stay competitive in a rapidly evolving job market.

At the end of the day, AI isn't something to fear—it's something to leverage. The more you explore AI tools, the more you'll see how they can make your life easier, whether in your personal life or career. The important thing is to stay curious and open-minded. The AI revolution isn't coming—it's already here, and it's making technology more accessible than ever before.

Now that we've dispelled the biggest myths about AI, it's time to dive deeper into how it's actively shaping industries, careers, and the way we live. Let's move forward with an open mind and see what AI can truly do.

Bonus: A Simple ChatGPT Prompt for Help With Breaking Down a Complex Topic

Prompt: (this is the command you give ChatGPT)

"Explain [insert complex topic] in simple terms, as if you were teaching it to a beginner. Use clear language and relatable examples to make it easy to understand."

Example Use:

"Explain quantum computing in simple terms, as if you were teaching it to a beginner. Use clear language and relatable examples to make it easy to understand."

This prompt encourages ChatGPT to break down complicated subjects into digestible pieces, making learning easier for beginners. You can customize it for any topic, from artificial intelligence to economics or science concepts.

3
AI AT USE IN OUR EVERYDAY LIVES

Imagine you're relaxing in your favorite spot, flipping through your social media, and you encounter a piece of digital art so stunning it leaves you breathless. Its vibrancy and complexity make you wonder if perhaps Leonardo da Vinci was resurrected to swap his brushes for a digital tablet. Yet, the truth is even more astonishing—this artwork wasn't even created by a real person. Welcome to the era of generative AI, where algorithms become the master artists and pixels their medium of choice.

Generative AI is like your quirky friend who can whip up a gourmet meal using leftovers from the fridge. It takes raw data—think numbers, words, even sounds—and transforms it into something entirely new and unique. At its core, generative AI uses machine learning to create content from data inputs, and it's taking the world by storm. Whether it's generating mesmerizing music, crafting compelling stories, or designing eye-catching images, generative AI is redefining creativity as we know it.

3.1 GENERATIVE AI AT WORK IN MUSIC & THE ARTS

Back in 2023, a song called Heart on My Sleeve quickly went viral and completely shocked the music world when it appeared to feature Drake and The Weeknd, only for fans to later realize that neither artist had actually recorded it. The song spread rapidly across streaming platforms, capturing attention for its strikingly realistic vocals and production, yet it was actually written by a generative AI and posted by an anonymous user on the internet.

The AI behind Heart on My Sleeve was able to mimic Drake's flow and The Weeknd's signature vocal style by analyzing vast amounts of their past music. Machine learning algorithms and deep neural networks pieced together an entirely new song, one that was convincing enough to fool thousands of listeners. This raises major questions about originality and ownership—if AI can generate new songs that are indistinguishable from real artists, who owns the rights to these creations? Additionally, with AI's ability to replicate voices, there is growing concern that this technology could be misused to produce misleading or harmful content, further blurring the lines between real and artificial artistry in music.

While some listeners were amazed at how realistic the song sounded, record labels were quick to shut it down, claiming copyright infringement. The song's removal highlights a growing battle between AI's creative potential and the legal and ethical concerns of using someone's likeness without permission. The legal side of AI in music is still in its early stages, leaving many unanswered questions. In the U.S., copyright law currently states that only humans can be considered the authors of creative works, meaning AI-generated music technically isn't protected.

But what happens when AI is used as a tool rather than the sole creator? Lawyers and music executives are scrambling to figure out how much human involvement is needed to claim ownership over an AI-generated song. With technology developing at lightning speed, legal experts worry that the law won't be able to keep up, making it difficult to protect artists while also allowing AI's creative possibilities to flourish.

AI's impact on music is already forcing the industry to rethink intellectual property and authenticity. Some see AI as an exciting tool that could revolutionize music production, allowing artists to experiment in new ways. Others worry that it could lead to a flood of soulless, automated music that diminishes the value of human creativity. Moving forward, record labels, artists, and lawmakers will need to collaborate on setting ethical and legal boundaries to ensure that AI enhances, rather than undermines, artistic integrity. Heart on My Sleeve may be one of the first high-profile cases of AI-related music controversy, but it certainly won't be the last.

In response, musicians and industry leaders have formed the Human Artistry Campaign, aiming to establish guidelines for AI in music. Their goal is to ensure that human creativity remains valued while also allowing AI to be used responsibly. Instead of relying on slow-moving laws, some artists believe musicians should lead the way in deciding how AI can be used in ethical ways. The debate over AI and music is just beginning, but one thing is clear: AI is here to stay, and finding a balance between technology and artistry will be one of the greatest challenges in the music industry moving forward.

None of this is meant to scare or worry you, but it's important to recognize the power of AI and the great responsibility that comes with it. Those who try to harness its powers as a shortcut to replace the best parts of humanity will likely see their successes be short-lived, but those of us who want to use it to free up menial tasks and help to create a better world along the way will be rewarded.

In the realm of visual arts, AI is also sparking a digital renaissance. Artists can now leverage AI to craft digital masterpieces at a mouse click, merging historical art styles with innovative designs. This fusion, akin to combining the insights of an art history professor with the creativity of an avant-garde artist, is producing art that is both recognizable and radically new. AI's role in the arts transcends mere imitation, propelling artists into new creative dimensions and enabling the creation of art that engages audiences in unprecedented ways.

3D modeling is another area where AI is flexing its creative muscles, turning virtual sculptures and environments into reality. Artists can now use AI to create intricate 3D models that were once painstakingly crafted by hand. Imagine sculpting a virtual statue with the precision of a master sculptor but without the marble dust. AI helps generate complex models more efficiently, allowing artists to focus on refining their work and experimenting with new concepts. This technology is like having a digital chisel, empowering artists to carve out new dimensions of creativity.

Consider AI-generated art. Imagine a computer program that can create stunning visuals, each more captivating than the last. AI tools like DALL-E are revolutionizing how we think about creativity. With a simple text prompt, DALL-E can conjure up images that are limited only by your imagination. Fancy a picture of a dog in a baseball cap drinking coffee in a Victorian parlor? DALL-E's got you covered. It's as if you've handed an easel to a computer and said, "Surprise me," and boy, does it deliver.

What's great about DALL-E is that you already get its services as a part of your package if you're a premium ChatGPT user, which at the time of this writing is $20 USD per month.

Other popular AI picture tools are Ideogram and Pikzels, where you can create a thumbnail or AI-generated picture in minutes solely from text prompts. Pikzel's technology is currently taking over the thumbnail market on YouTube for content creators, and the customization that it provides is simply incredible.

Generative AI isn't just about making cool images or writing fancy text—it's changing the way we design, market, and innovate. In product design, AI can generate ideas that human creators might never think of, like a car with unexpected but useful features. In marketing, it helps create personalized ads that speak directly to individual preferences, making brand interactions feel more engaging and relevant. Instead of one-size-fits-all campaigns, companies can use AI to tailor content that feels like it was made just for you.

If you are eager to explore generative AI for yourself, there are plenty of beginner-friendly tools to try. Platforms like DALL-E and ChatGPT (both from OpenAI) let you create art, write stories, or brainstorm ideas with AI's help—no tech degree required. It's like having a creative assistant who works at lightning speed, helping bring your ideas to life. And the impact goes far beyond creativity. In industries like fashion, AI is designing virtual clothing, reducing waste by eliminating unnecessary production. In gaming, AI-generated environments and characters make every experience unique, adapting in real-time to player choices. Whether you're designing, marketing, or just having fun, generative AI is reshaping what's possible.

As we delve deeper into the realm of generative AI, its potential seems boundless. This technology is not just about creating content; it's about reshaping how we think about creativity itself. In a world where algorithms are the new creators, the possibilities are as endless as the data they draw from. So, whether you're an aspiring artist, a budding writer, or someone who just loves a good story, generative AI invites you to imagine, create, and explore like never before.

3.2 EXPLORING NATURAL LANGUAGE PROCESSING (NLP) AND AI

Imagine sitting in a bustling café, trying to decipher a foreign menu with the help of your trusty translation app. It feels a bit like magic, doesn't it? That's natural language processing (NLP) at play, making computers understand and respond to human languages. Think of NLP as the linguistic bridge between humans and machines. It's what enables your phone to transform spoken commands into actions or convert text from one language to another. Whether it's detecting sarcasm in a tweet or translating an email from a colleague in Tokyo, NLP is the unsung hero of our digital interactions.

One fascinating aspect of NLP is sentiment analysis, which is like giving computers a crash course in emotional intelligence. Imagine a computer reading a product review and figuring out whether the customer is thrilled or disappointed. It's like watching a robot try to understand why humans cry. Another vital role NLP plays is in language translation. Gone are the days of fumbling with phrase-books. Now, apps can seamlessly convert your words into another language, ensuring you didn't accidentally order a plate of snails when you meant to ask for steak. This ability to understand and translate languages is reshaping our world, breaking down barriers, and fostering communication across continents.

NLP's real importance lies in enhancing how we interact with technology. Consider chatbots, which seemed bizarre several years ago, but now we're all pretty much used to them. These AI-driven customer service reps are ready 24/7, providing instant support without the need for a coffee break. They can sift through your queries and offer solutions right away. Then there are voice assistants, those friendly voices you summon with a simple "Hey, Siri" or "Okay, Google." They understand spoken commands, helping you set reminders, play music, or find out if it's going to rain, all while you're busy cooking dinner or even jogging.

For those eager to dabble in NLP, there are beginner-friendly tools at your disposal. Google Cloud Natural Language lets you analyze text content, making it a perfect playground for those curious about sentiment analysis and entity recognition. Want to translate languages with the finesse of a seasoned diplomat? IBM Watson Language Translator has got you covered.

Consider the practical applications of NLP in our everyday lives. Social media monitoring is a big one. Companies use NLP to gauge brand sentiment, analyzing tweets and posts to understand how customers feel about their products. It's like having an ear to the ground, listening to the chatter, and picking up on trends before they become mainstream. In healthcare, NLP plays a crucial role in interpreting patient inquiries and ensuring clear communication between healthcare providers and patients. Imagine a system that helps doctors and nurses quickly understand patient concerns, streamlining the process and improving care.

NLP is more than just a tech buzzword; it's a transformative force reshaping how we interact with our digital world. It's the silent partner in our devices, working tirelessly to make our interactions smoother, smarter, and more intuitive. Whether you're ordering lunch in a foreign land or chatting with your digital assistant, NLP is there, quietly making sure everything goes off without a hitch.

3.3 AI IN AUGMENTED REALITY: THE INTERSECTION OF REAL AND DIGITAL WORLDS

Imagine you're walking through a bustling city, your phone in hand, and suddenly, your screen lights up with digital arrows guiding you to the best sushi spot in town. That's augmented reality (AR) in action—blending digital elements with the real world to enhance your surroundings. Whether through AR glasses or a smartphone, AR is transforming everyday experiences, making the physical world more interactive around us. Picture shopping for furniture and instantly seeing how a couch fits in your living room before you buy it. In retail, AR is revolutionizing the shopping experience by offering virtual try-ons for clothing and accessories. No more guessing if those sunglasses will suit your face shape; just point your phone at your reflection and try them on virtually. AR overlays digital content onto real-world settings, turning imagination into visualization and making tasks easier, more engaging, and even fun.

AI is what makes AR truly intelligent. AI-powered object recognition helps AR apps "see" the world accurately, ensuring digital elements are placed in the right spots. Gesture recognition allows users to interact with AR using simple hand movements—like waving away a notification or rotating a 3D model. This AI-enhanced interactivity makes AR feel intuitive, bridging the gap between technology and natural human interaction. From virtual try-ons in retail to interactive learning experiences in education, AI-powered AR is changing how we shop, study, and engage with digital content.

AR has also transformed gaming and entertainment, blurring the lines between the virtual and physical worlds. The launch of Pokémon GO in 2016 was just the beginning—now, AR is used for tabletop games, sports training, and fully immersive experiences that adjust dynamically based on player behavior. AI-driven AR learns from users, delivering smarter, more personalized gameplay that evolves in real time. Whether revolutionizing retail, education, or entertainment, AI-powered AR is reshaping the way we interact with technology, making everyday experiences richer and more engaging.

For those eager to explore AR, there are accessible platforms to get you started. Apple's ARKit offers a playground for developing AR experiences on iOS devices, allowing beginners to create apps that blend the digital with the real. Meanwhile, Google ARCore provides similar capabilities for Android users, enabling the creation of AR applications that can run on a wide range of devices. These platforms are designed to be user-friendly, offering a toolkit for creative exploration without requiring deep technical knowledge. Whether you're a developer dreaming of the next big app or simply curious about the possibilities of AR, these tools open up a world of creative potential right at your fingertips.

3.4 CLOUD COMPUTING AND AI: LEVERAGING THE POWER OF THE CLOUD

Think of your computer like a librarian trying to manage an ever-growing collection of books. Now imagine that same librarian has access to a massive digital library that never runs out of space and processes information at lightning speed. That's cloud computing—a virtual powerhouse that supports AI by providing the storage and processing power it needs. AI thrives on data, and cloud computing acts as its foundation, storing everything from social media trends to complex scientific models while ensuring AI can access and analyze it instantly.

The combination of cloud computing and AI is a perfect match. Cloud services let AI systems scale up effortlessly, like expanding a dining table when more guests arrive. Instead of being limited by your computer's hardware, AI can tap into cloud resources as needed, making it easier for businesses, researchers, and even casual users to experiment with AI without needing powerful machines. Another advantage is accessibility—AI tools hosted in the cloud are available to anyone with an internet connection anywhere in the world. Whether you're a student, entrepreneur, or hobbyist, cloud computing ensures you can explore AI's potential without expensive equipment.

For beginners interested in cloud-based AI, there are easy-to-use platforms ready to explore. Amazon Web Services (AWS) offers AI and machine learning tools that help users build, train, and test AI models from any device. Microsoft Azure AI also provides cloud-based solutions that cater to both beginners and advanced developers, removing the need for complex hardware setups. These platforms make AI more accessible than ever, allowing users to experiment, collaborate, and create innovative projects without needing a deep technical background. From real-time analytics that helps businesses track trends to AI-powered virtual collaboration tools, cloud computing and AI are transforming the way we work, learn, and connect.

3.5 INTERNET OF THINGS AND AI: MAKING SMART DEVICES SMARTER

Imagine waking up to a fresh cup of coffee already brewed while your thermostat adjusts to the perfect morning temperature. That's the magic of the Internet of Things (IoT), a network of smart devices that communicate and work together to make life easier. Think of it as a group chat for your appliances, where everything from your fridge to your home lights can share information and automate everyday tasks. These devices aren't just about convenience—they improve efficiency, save energy, and give you back precious time to focus on what matters most.

Beyond smart homes, IoT is revolutionizing industries. In factories, IoT sensors monitor machinery, predicting maintenance needs before breakdowns occur—like a built-in warning system that prevents costly repairs. AI plays a major role in making IoT even smarter. It analyzes data from sensors, helping businesses improve efficiency, reduce waste, and make better decisions. In smart buildings, AI optimizes lighting and heating systems based on usage patterns, cutting down energy costs without sacrificing comfort. It's like having an intelligent assistant constantly fine-tuning your surroundings for maximum efficiency.

For those curious about building their own IoT projects, platforms like Google Cloud IoT and Arduino IoT Cloud make it easier than ever. These tools let users connect devices, analyze data, and even incorporate AI for smarter automation. Whether you're a hobbyist experimenting with a DIY smart home setup or a business looking to streamline operations, these platforms provide the foundation to bring IoT ideas to life—no advanced tech skills required.

The combination of IoT and AI is changing the way we live, work, and even take care of our health. Smart agriculture uses IoT sensors to monitor soil conditions and weather, while AI processes the data to help farmers maximize crop yields. In healthcare, wearable devices track vital signs and use AI to detect potential health risks early. From improving industries to making daily routines smoother, IoT and AI are shaping a world where technology not only connects but collaborates, creating a smarter and more intuitive future.

Now that we've got all the basics covered, we can get to the moment you've all been waiting for: AI tools and how you can begin using them in your daily life.

Key Takeaways from Chapter 3

- **Generative AI is redefining creativity.** Tools like DALL-E, Ideogram, and Pikzels are making it possible for anyone to create professional-quality art, text, and even video thumbnails with simple text prompts. AI is no longer just analyzing information—it's creating new content and reshaping industries from marketing to entertainment.
- **AI-generated music could be used to falsely represent artists and spread misinformation**. There's concern that AI could lower artistic standards, leading to generic, soulless music. Artists and industry leaders are pushing for ethical AI guidelines in music. AI's impact on music is inevitable, but responsible usage will hopefully determine its future role and make it a good one.
- **Natural Language Processing (NLP)** helps AI understand human language. Whether it's real-time translation, voice assistants like Siri and Alexa, or customer service chatbots, AI is bridging the gap between humans and machines. NLP is making communication across languages and cultures seamless, and businesses are using sentiment analysis to track customer opinions in real-time.

- **Augmented Reality (AR)** is merging digital and physical worlds. Whether you're trying on virtual clothes, shopping for furniture with AR previews, or playing immersive AR video games, AI is powering new experiences that change how we interact with the world around us. AI-driven AR is also being used in education and training, creating highly interactive learning experiences.
- **Cloud computing is the backbone of AI.** AI relies on vast amounts of data and computing power, and cloud platforms like AWS, Microsoft Azure, and Google Cloud are making it possible for businesses and individuals to tap into advanced AI without needing expensive hardware. This accessibility is democratizing AI, allowing more people to use and benefit from it.
- **The Internet of Things (IoT) and AI are making smart devices even smarter.** From self-adjusting thermostats to wearables that monitor your health in real time, AI-enhanced IoT devices are creating a world where our technology adapts to us rather than the other way around. In industries like healthcare and agriculture, AI-powered IoT is driving efficiency, optimizing resources, and improving outcomes.

Bonus: A Simple ChatGPT Prompt for Brainstorming Ideas

Prompt: "I need creative ideas for a [type of project]. It should be engaging, unique, and suitable for [target audience]. Can you suggest different angles, themes, or approaches I could explore?"

For example:

"I need creative ideas for a social media marketing campaign. It should be engaging, unique, and suitable for small business owners. Can you suggest different angles, themes, or approaches I could explore?"

This prompt gives ChatGPT enough direction to generate useful ideas while leaving room for creativity. You can also refine it by adding more details about your goals, preferred tone, or constraints.

4
SIMPLE AI TOOLS TO GET YOU STARTED

Imagine AI as a vast ocean, teeming with possibilities and opportunities, yet you're standing at the shore wondering how to dive in without being swept away by the currents. Fear not! This chapter is your life raft, guiding you through the initial splash as you explore the world of AI tools tailored for beginners. Navigating this digital sea needn't be daunting. Like picking the right gear for fishing (nobody wants to catch a boot), choosing the proper AI tools requires a bit of know-how. But once you know what to look for, you'll be reeling in the benefits in no time.

When considering AI tools, keep an eye out for user interface simplicity. Think of it as the friendly stewardess pointing out emergency exits—clear, straightforward, and easy to follow. A tool with an intuitive design means you spend less time scratching your head and more time actually using it. For instance, a drag-and-drop feature in an app can save you from staring blankly at a screen filled with code. Comprehensive support is another must-have. Look for tools that come with tutorials and customer service, akin to having a tour guide on your tech journey, ready to answer questions and provide directions. This support ensures that when you hit a snag, you've got a helping hand (or a helpful FAQ) to get you back on track.

Now, let's take a peek into the treasure trove of AI tools available to beginners. Whether you're looking to boost productivity or polish your grammar, there's a tool designed just for you. AI-powered productivity apps like Trello, now with AI enhancements, help you organize tasks with the finesse of a personal assistant who never forgets. Need to write an email without sounding like a robot? Language processing tools like Grammarly are your go-to. They offer real-time suggestions to strengthen your writing, transforming your prose from 'meh' to 'marvelous' without breaking a sweat. These tools are designed to make your life easier, not add to your to-do list.

Among the pantheon of beginner-friendly AI tools, a few stand out as household names. Google Assistant and Google Translate are like the dynamic duo of digital helpers. Google Assistant can set reminders, play your favorite tunes, and even tell you a joke if you're in need of a chuckle. Meanwhile, Google Translate breaks down language barriers faster than you can say "bonjour." Microsoft also joins the fray with Cortana and Power BI. Cortana is your AI sidekick, helping you navigate the digital landscape, while Power BI offers powerful data visualization tools to make sense of those pesky spreadsheets. It's like having a digital Swiss army knife at your disposal.

Of course, the cost of these digital wonders can vary, so it's wise to weigh your options. Some tools are free, offering basic features without demanding a dime. Others operate on a subscription model, akin to a gym membership for your brain, providing access to premium features for a monthly fee. Understanding what you need and what you're willing to spend is key to finding the right fit. Consider the value of features offered against their cost, ensuring you're getting the best bang for your buck. After all, you wouldn't pay for a full buffet if you're only stopping by for the salad bar.

Interactive Exercise: AI Tool Matchmaker

Let's find your AI soulmate! Consider what tasks you need help with: Is it organizing your schedule? Improving your writing? Analyzing data? List three tasks you'd like to optimize with AI. Next, research an AI tool for each task, noting its features, user interface, and cost. Compare your findings and choose the tool that best fits your needs. This exercise helps you select the right tool and familiarizes you with the process of evaluating tech options—an invaluable skill in today's digital age.

Embarking on this exploration of AI tools can be as exhilarating as discovering a new hobby. With the proper tools in hand, you'll be equipped to enhance your productivity, streamline tasks, and maybe even impress your friends with your newfound tech-savviness.

4.1 OVERCOMING FEAR: BUILDING CONFIDENCE IN YOUR ABILITY TO LEARN AI

When you approach AI with an open mind, mistakes become valuable lessons rather than setbacks. Much like learning to ride a bike, you'll probably stumble a few times before you find your balance. Every AI tool you use will likely have a little bit of a learning curve in the beginning, so celebrate those small victories, whether grasping a new concept or successfully using an AI tool to get what you want. Each step forward is progress, and recognizing your achievements along the way boosts your confidence and helps keep you motivated.

Hearing about others who have conquered their AI fears can also be incredibly inspiring. Take, for example, Sarah Burton, a mid-career professional who initially viewed AI as a threat to her job. Instead of retreating, she decided to learn about AI and how it could complement her skills. Through online courses and community workshops, Sarah not only enhanced her career prospects on her resume but also became an advocate for AI literacy in her workplace. Her story shows that with curiosity and determination, anyone can adapt and thrive in an AI-enhanced world. Testimonials like Sarah's remind us that AI isn't a closed door but a pathway to new opportunities.

Building confidence in AI learning isn't about diving into the deep end without a life vest. It's about setting achievable goals and breaking the learning process into manageable tasks. Start small, maybe by exploring a basic AI tool or reading an introductory article. As you gain confidence, you can gradually tackle more complex topics. Joining an AI learning community like "Learn AI Together" on a messaging app like Discord can also provide a supportive environment where you can share experiences, ask questions, and learn from others. Whether it's an online forum or a local meetup, these communities offer encouragement and camaraderie, making the learning process less daunting and more enjoyable.

In this journey, remember that perfection isn't the goal—progress is. Embrace the process, relish the discoveries, and don't shy away from asking for help when needed. AI might seem like a complex puzzle, but with patience and persistence, you'll find that it's a puzzle you can solve. And who knows? You might even find yourself enjoying the challenge, unlocking new skills and knowledge that enrich your personal and professional life.

Consistency is key when it comes to learning anything new. Think of daily practice as the gentle nudge your brain needs to retain information. By engaging with AI concepts regularly, you're reinforcing knowledge and building confidence. Establishing routines is like setting your brain's cruise control—after a while, it becomes second nature. Whether it's playing around with Alexa during breakfast or exploring AI articles during lunch breaks, these small habits compound over time, leading to significant progress. And let's be honest, there's something satisfying about ticking off a daily study session on your to-do calendar.

4.2 USING CHATGPT TO IMPROVE EMAIL WRITING

Ah, emails. Those digital missives that clutter our inboxes to the brink. Whether you're writing to your boss, sending a friendly note to a colleague, or reaching out to a distant relative, crafting the perfect email can sometimes feel like a Herculean task. Enter ChatGPT, your personal editor, ready to polish those emails until they shine. Imagine having an editor who doesn't judge your grammar mistakes and actually enjoys sifting through your misspelled words. That's ChatGPT for you. With a simple prompt like, "Can you help me refine this email to make it more professional?" ChatGPT becomes your instant copy editor, tidying up your text by fixing grammar hiccups and smoothing out awkward phrasing.

But ChatGPT doesn't stop at just cleaning up your prose. Oh no, this AI assistant is also a master of style. You can ask, "Could you make this email sound more friendly?" and watch as your message transforms from stiff and formal to warm and engaging. Suddenly, what was once a cold, robotic note becomes a delightful conversation starter, complete with a personalized touch that makes your recipient feel like you're right there in the room with them. And if you need to switch gears and adopt a more formal tone, ChatGPT is ready to suit up and deliver the gravitas your email demands.

Now, for those of you who dread the thought of starting from scratch, ChatGPT can help ease that initial writer's block with prompts like, "Draft an email requesting feedback on a recent project." With just a few words, ChatGPT provides a solid framework, allowing you to focus on the content while it handles the structure. It's like having a co-pilot who navigates the tricky parts while you enjoy the view. This assistance is particularly handy when you're up against a deadline and need to send out multiple emails in a short amount of time. ChatGPT gives you the boost you need to get those emails out the door without breaking a sweat.

Let's not overlook the beauty of a well-organized email. You know, the kind that doesn't require a map to navigate. ChatGPT can help you with prompts like, "Organize this email with bullet points for clarity." By breaking down your message into concise, digestible sections, ChatGPT ensures your main points stand out. This approach makes your emails easier to read and enhances engagement, keeping your recipient's attention from start to finish.

And for those who find themselves sending the same email over and over again, ChatGPT can assist in creating templates with prompts like, "Design an email template for scheduling meetings." These templates save you time, ensuring consistency and professionalism in every message. Whether it's an out-of-office reply or a client follow-up, having a template at the ready means you spend less time typing and more time tackling other tasks.

Of course, no email is complete without a memorable sign-off, and ChatGPT excels in crafting those final touches. With a prompt like, "Suggest a unique sign-off for a friendly email," you can elevate your goodbyes from mundane to memorable. Instead of the usual "Best regards," you might find yourself signing off with a creative flourish that leaves a lasting impression. Your emails will end on a high note, ensuring your recipient remembers you long after they've hit reply.

And there you have it—a trusty sidekick in your email writing endeavors. From grammar guru to style savant, ChatGPT is ready to tackle whatever email challenge you throw its way. Whether you're crafting the perfect apology note, extending a warm invitation, or simply catching up with an old friend, ChatGPT has you covered. With its ability to enhance clarity, inject personality, and streamline your messaging, ChatGPT transforms your emails into polished gems that dazzle with every click.

So next time you find yourself staring at a blank screen, wondering how to start that daunting email, remember that ChatGPT is just a prompt away, ready to assist with a touch of humor and a dash of style. Whether you're a seasoned email veteran or just getting started in the world of digital communication, ChatGPT is your go-to resource for crafting emails that make an impact. With its help, you'll navigate the world of email writing with confidence, charm, and efficiency, ensuring your messages always hit the mark.

4.3 AUTOMATING REPETITIVE TASKS WITH AI: SIMPLIFYING YOUR WORKFLOW

Let's face it: nobody dreams of spending their day sorting through a mountain of emails or manually entering data into spreadsheets. Luckily, AI is here to rescue you from this digital drudgery, swooping in like a caped crusader armed with algorithms instead of a utility belt. The first step is identifying which mundane tasks in your daily routine can be gracefully handed over to our AI friends. Sorting through emails, for instance, is a prime candidate. AI can organize your inbox, categorizing messages faster than you can say "spam filter." And then there's data entry. No more squinting at tiny cells in spreadsheets—AI can autofill these for you with the precision of a seasoned accountant.

Now, let's elaborate on some of the trusty sidekicks available to help automate these tasks. Meet Zapier and IFTTT (If This Then That), two stalwarts in the world of workflow automation. Think of Zapier as your personal digital assistant, connecting your favorite apps and streamlining workflows through integrations. Whether it's automatically saving email attachments to cloud storage or posting tweets from your blog, Zapier has got you covered. IFTTT, on the other hand, is like a crafty magician, creating simple automation scripts that perform tasks based on "if this happens, then do that" logic. It's perfect for setting up chains of events, like automatically turning off your smart lights when you leave the house.

Setting up automation is simpler than assembling a piece of flat-pack furniture (and with fewer screws left over). Start by creating workflows, also known as trigger-action pairs. In plain English, this means defining what action should occur when a specific event happens. For example, "If I receive an email with an attachment, then save it to Google Drive." Once you've set up these triggers, it's crucial to test your automation to ensure they're functioning as intended. This is where the fun part comes in—watching your inbox magically sort itself while you sip on your morning smoothie.

The benefits of embracing workflow automation are as clear as a crystal ball. First off, there's the time savings. By offloading repetitive tasks to AI, you free up precious hours for strategic work. It's like hiring a personal assistant who doesn't require lunch breaks or a salary. Not to mention, automation dramatically reduces human error. No more typos from tired eyes or accidentally deleting important data because you were daydreaming about your next vacation. With AI, you can trust that tasks are executed accurately every time, giving you peace of mind and a little extra time to daydream guilt-free.

4.4 USING AI FOR DATA ANALYSIS

AI-driven data analysis can take raw numbers and turn them into valuable insights with just a few clicks. At its core, it's about identifying patterns and trends that aren't immediately obvious—like digging through a messy drawer to find which exact item you need. The process starts with organizing and cleaning up your data to make it usable. Once that's done, AI steps in, scanning for trends, anomalies, and connections that might go unnoticed. Whether it's spotting a decline in sales or identifying customer preferences, AI helps reveal the bigger picture, making complex data easier to understand.

Getting started with AI-powered data analysis is simpler than it sounds. First, you'll need a tool like IBM Watson or Tableau, both of which offer beginner-friendly interfaces. Once you've uploaded your data, visualization tools create charts and graphs that help bring the numbers to life—almost like turning a dense spreadsheet into an easy-to-read comic strip. Visualizing data allows you to quickly identify trends and outliers, making decision-making faster and more effective. The best part? AI doesn't just crunch numbers—it helps you see the story behind them.

The biggest benefits of AI in data analysis are speed, accuracy, and clarity. AI can process massive datasets in seconds, eliminating the hours of manual work that used to be required. It also reduces human error, ensuring that your findings are as precise as possible. But even with AI, interpreting data still requires a bit of human insight. Think of your findings as puzzle pieces—each one is important, but you need to fit them together to see the full picture. When presenting your analysis, focus on telling a clear, compelling story with charts and graphs that make your insights easy to understand. Whether you're using AI to improve sales, optimize business operations, or enhance customer satisfaction, the key is turning data into actionable decisions that drive results.

4.5 ONLINE AI COMMUNITIES: JOINING THE CONVERSATION

Joining an online AI community connects you with like-minded enthusiasts who are eager to explore topics together. These forums serve as dynamic learning centers where expert insights meet beginner curiosity. They offer a wealth of knowledge from experienced professionals ready to provide guidance when needed. Moreover, these communities are not just about learning; they're venues for networking, sparking collaborations, and creating valuable connections that could propel your projects forward. Here, you'll discover your 'AI tribe,' a group equally passionate about decoding complex challenges and grasping new concepts.

Take Reddit's r/MachineLearning, for instance. This forum is a hotspot for engaging in in-depth AI discussions, where daily threads cover everything from cutting-edge research to practical applications. It's like a never-ending conference, with the only requirement being a curious mind. AI Stack Exchange, on the other hand, is your go-to for seeking answers to technical questions. It's a treasure trove of knowledge where you can post queries and receive detailed responses from experienced practitioners. Think of it as a massive Q&A session where every participant is eager to help you succeed. These platforms are invaluable resources, providing you with the latest updates, trends, and developments in the AI world.

Participating in online AI communities elevates your learning beyond solo study. Sharing knowledge in these forums is like tending a communal garden—every interaction nurtures growth. This collective effort not only keeps you updated with AI's rapid advancements but also deepens your understanding. Teaching and discussing AI concepts within these communities proves that imparting knowledge is just as valuable as acquiring it.

Key Takeaways from Chapter 4:

- **Start with User-Friendly AI Tools** – Many AI platforms are designed for beginners with simple interfaces, step-by-step tutorials, and drag-and-drop functionality. Tools like Grammarly for writing, Trello for task management, and Google Assistant for personal organization make AI accessible to everyone—no coding required.
- **Leverage AI for Productivity & Creativity** – AI can help automate time-consuming tasks, generate creative ideas, and optimize workflows. Whether it's using ChatGPT to brainstorm content, Zapier to connect your favorite apps, or an AI-powered email assistant to draft up responses and various email templates to save for later, these tools help free up valuable time.

- **Understand Cost vs. Benefit** – Some AI tools are free, while others operate on a subscription basis. Consider what features are essential for your needs and whether paying for premium access makes sense. Just like a gym membership, investing in the right AI tools can be worth it if you use them consistently.
- **Confidence Comes with Practice** – Like learning any new skill, using AI effectively takes time and experimentation. The more you engage with AI, the more comfortable you'll become. Even small daily interactions—whether asking Siri for the weather or using AI to draft an email—help to build confidence and familiarity.
- **Find the Right AI for You** – Everyone has different needs, so the best AI tool for one person may not be the best for another. Use the "AI Tool Matchmaker" exercise to identify which AI applications align with your personal or professional goals. Whether it's streamlining your work tasks, improving efficiency, or exploring creative projects, AI can be a valuable asset.

Getting started with AI doesn't mean overhauling your entire routine—it simply means integrating smart, efficient tools into your daily life. As AI technology continues to evolve, staying curious and open to new possibilities will allow you to make the most of these powerful innovations. Now that you have a strong foundation in beginner-friendly AI tools, the next step is learning how to apply AI to improve your career, boost your skills, and stay competitive in the ever-changing job market.

Bonus: A Simple ChatGPT Prompt for Better Email Writing

Prompt:

"Write a professional email to [recipient's name or title] regarding [topic]. The email should be polite, concise, and clearly communicate [key message or request]. Include a greeting, a short introduction, the main purpose of

the email, and a polite closing. Keep the tone [formal/friendly/helpful] and ensure proper grammar and clarity."

Example Usage:

"Write a professional email to a client regarding an upcoming project deadline. The email should be polite and concise, and any required next steps should be clearly communicated. Include a greeting, a short introduction, the main purpose of the email, and a polite closing. Keep the tone professional and ensure proper grammar and clarity."

This prompt ensures that ChatGPT generates a well-structured email while allowing the user to customize it to fit their needs.

From here, you can just copy and paste the response into your email, change it around to your liking, and voilà. Time saved.

MAKE A DIFFERENCE WITH YOUR REVIEW

UNLOCKING THE POWER OF GENEROSITY

"At the end of the day, it's not about what you have or even what you've accomplished. It's about who you've lifted up, who you've made better. It's about what you've given back." – Denzel Washington

People who take a moment to help others—without expecting anything in return—make the world a better place. So, let's do something great together!

Would you help someone just like you—curious about AI but unsure where to start?

YOUR REVIEW COULD CHANGE SOMEONE'S AI JOURNEY

My goal with *AI Essentials for Beginners* was simple: to make learning AI easy, fun, and practical. AI is transforming the world faster than ever, and I want more people to understand it, use it, and benefit from it—whether for work, business, or everyday life.

But here's the thing—most people pick up a book because someone like **you** left a review.

A quick review helps someone else take their first step into AI. And who knows? That one step could change everything. Your review could help...

✓ A small business owner use AI to work smarter and grow faster.

✓ An entrepreneur find new ways to turn their ideas into reality.

✔ A job seeker land their dream role by understanding AI's impact on hiring.

✔ A curious learner gain confidence in an AI-driven world.

✔ An older professional not fall behind the curve when it comes to AI and technology

LEAVING A REVIEW IS SIMPLE & FREE

If this book helped you in any way, you can pay it forward by leaving a quick review. It takes less than a minute but makes a huge difference.

📍 To make a difference, simply scan the QR code below and leave a review:

https://www.amazon.com/review/review-your-purchases/?asin=B0F22TGXXW

If you love helping others, you're my kind of person. Thank you for being part of this journey!

– Kyle Lindemann

5
USING AI TO LEVEL UP AT WORK

This is the biggest AI-related topic that people in my everyday life have had the most questions about, and rightfully so. It's one thing to be genuinely curious about AI and how it's changing the world around us, but many of you are eager to know more about how it's directly applicable to your life and how you can use it to your advantage in your career. In the following chapters, we will assess how you can use AI to become more efficient at the office, how AI can help you become more skilled and competitive in your profession, and how AI can even improve your quality of life at home.

Whether or not the professions listed below directly align with your current career path, this chapter offers valuable insights for everyone. If these fields don't match your own, consider this section a chance to explore the broader implications of AI on the global job market, or head on over to Chapter 6. However, if you're actively engaged in one of these professions, contemplating a career shift, a student, or simply intrigued by the transformative power of AI across various job sectors, then you'll find this chapter particularly enlightening.

By the year 2025, artificial intelligence has become a cornerstone of innovation in numerous industries, dramatically enhancing efficiency, automating routine tasks, and fundamentally altering job descriptions. Below, we will delve into many of the job fields being the most profoundly affected by the advent of AI technologies.

An Important Disclaimer: Before you begin diving into the usage of AI tools at your place of work, make sure they are approved and allowed, of course. Your Employee Handbook is probably a good place to start before having a conversation with your direct supervisor.

5.1 AI TOOLS FOR ACCOUNTING AND FINANCE

In 2025, AI isn't just a tool—it's an essential asset for accountants looking to sharpen their skills and stay competitive in an increasingly automated industry. AI can help streamline financial reporting, detect fraud patterns, and even generate insights for better decision-making. Tools like ChatGPT can quickly explain complex tax codes, summarize regulatory updates, and even draft client emails, freeing up time for higher-level analysis. AI-powered software such as Intuit's QuickBooks AI, Xero, and Oracle NetSuite are making bookkeeping and forecasting more efficient, meaning accountants who embrace these tools will work smarter, not harder. By integrating AI into daily workflows, accountants can improve accuracy and expand their roles from number-crunchers to strategic financial advisors.

To stay ahead of the curve, accountants can pursue AI-focused certifications that highlight their ability to navigate emerging technologies. In 2025, some of the most valuable certifications include the Certified Management Accountant (CMA), which now incorporates AI-driven financial planning, and the Certified Information Systems Auditor (CISA), which focuses on AI and cybersecurity in financial auditing. The AI in Accounting and Finance Certificate from the AICPA (American Institute of Certified Public Accountants) is another great way to showcase your expertise in AI-powered automation, data analytics, and risk assessment. Listing these credentials on a résumé signals to employers and clients that an accountant is not just keeping up with industry trends but leading the charge in modern financial technology.

Beyond earning certifications, accountants can use AI to become more analytical and proactive in their roles. AI-driven platforms can automate repetitive tasks like invoice reconciliation and tax preparation, allowing accountants to focus on more strategic areas such as financial forecasting and fraud prevention. Learning how to work with AI-powered Robotic Process Automation (RPA) can give accountants a serious edge, enabling them to accelerate tedious processes while reducing errors. Additionally, staying updated on AI-driven data visualization tools like Tableau and Power BI can enhance reporting skills and help accountants turn raw financial data into compelling, easy-to-understand insights for clients or stakeholders. By embracing AI, accountants don't just stay relevant —they position themselves as leaders in a field that's rapidly evolving.

5.2 AI TOOLS FOR FINANCIAL PLANNING/INVESTING

AI has become a game-changer in financial planning, offering powerful tools that help advisors make more informed decisions, personalize client strategies, and automate routine tasks. For a middle-aged financial planner looking to stay ahead, AI-driven platforms like Wealthfront, eMoney Advisor, and Orion Advisor Solutions can analyze vast amounts of financial data to generate predictive insights. AI chatbots and virtual assistants can streamline client communication, answer common questions, and free up time for deeper, high-value consultations. With AI handling portfolio rebalancing, tax optimization, and market trend analysis in real-time, financial planners can focus on building stronger client relationships and providing tailored financial strategies that keep them ahead of the competition.

To further boost their credentials, financial planners can earn certifications that demonstrate their proficiency in AI-driven financial tools and data analytics. The Certified Financial Planner (CFP) designation remains essential, but additional certifications like the Chartered Financial Analyst (CFA) Institute's Certificate in ESG Investing and the Financial Data Professional (FDP) Charter are becoming increasingly valuable in an AI-powered world. The AI in Wealth Management Certificate from the CFA Institute or the FinTech Certificate from MIT Sloan can highlight expertise in leveraging technology to optimize financial planning as well. Adding these credentials to a résumé signals to both clients and employers that a financial planner is not just keeping up with industry trends but actively mastering them.

Beyond certifications, financial planners who embrace AI can position themselves as forward-thinking strategists in a rapidly evolving industry. AI-driven predictive analytics tools can help advisors forecast market movements and adjust portfolios accordingly, reducing risk and maximizing returns. Mastering AI-enhanced financial modeling tools like Bloomberg Terminal AI or Morningstar Direct can provide more profound insights into asset performance and economic trends. Additionally, learning how to use AI-powered risk assessment software can help advisors build more resilient, adaptive financial plans for their clients. By integrating AI into their practice, financial planners don't just improve efficiency—they transform their role into that of a trusted, high-tech advisor in an increasingly digital world.

5.3 AI TOOLS FOR MARKETING/ADVERTISING

AI has completely reshaped marketing and advertising, turning data-driven insights into precision-targeted campaigns that drive real engagement. For professionals in this space, embracing AI tools like ChatGPT for content generation, Midjourney for AI-powered visuals, and Jasper AI for ad copywriting can significantly streamline workflow and boost creativity. AI-driven analytics platforms such as Google's Performance Max, HubSpot AI, and Sprinklr can automate audience segmentation, optimize ad spending, and generate predictive insights that refine marketing strategies in real-time. Marketing professionals who harness these tools effectively won't just work faster—they'll work smarter, ensuring that every campaign is backed by data-driven decision-making and tailored messaging.

To stay competitive, marketing and advertising professionals can pursue AI and digital marketing certifications that demonstrate expertise in the latest technology-driven strategies. Certifications like Google's AI-Powered Digital Marketing Certificate, HubSpot's AI for Marketing and Sales Certification, and the IBM Applied AI Professional Certificate can help professionals showcase their ability to leverage AI tools in branding, ad optimization, and consumer behavior analysis. For those working in programmatic advertising or paid media, earning the Meta Certified Digital Marketing Associate or the AI-Powered Advertising Certificate from the American Marketing Association (AMA) can boost credibility and open doors to new opportunities. Adding these certifications to a résumé not only proves technical proficiency, but also signals a forward-thinking approach in an industry that's evolving at lightning speed.

Beyond certifications, the most successful marketing professionals will be those who embrace AI-powered personalization and automation to craft more engaging campaigns for customers. AI-driven predictive analytics can forecast consumer trends and optimize campaign performance, while natural language processing (NLP) tools can analyze sentiment and adjust messaging accordingly. Professionals who master AI-enhanced customer journey mapping through tools like Adobe Sensei or Salesforce Einstein can deliver hyper-personalized experiences that resonate with audiences.

5.4 AI TOOLS FOR SOFTWARE ENGINEERING & IT

For software engineers and IT professionals, AI is both a game-changer and a necessity. AI-powered tools like GitHub Copilot, Tabnine, and Codeium assist developers by suggesting optimized code, debugging errors, and even automating repetitive coding tasks. Meanwhile, AI-driven cybersecurity platforms help IT teams detect vulnerabilities in real-time, and machine learning algorithms optimize cloud computing infrastructure. To stay ahead, professionals should integrate AI-driven DevOps workflows, automate software testing with AI, and leverage predictive analytics for system performance optimization. Those who embrace these tools aren't just keeping up—they're setting the pace.

To future-proof their careers, software engineers and IT specialists should invest in AI-focused certifications. Some of the most sought-after include the Microsoft Certified: Azure AI Engineer Associate, AWS Certified Machine Learning – Specialty, and Google Cloud Professional Machine Learning Engineer. Additionally, IT professionals can benefit from AI-centric cybersecurity credentials like the Certified AI Security Specialist (CAISS) or the CompTIA AI+ certification, which focuses on AI applications in IT environments. These credentials enhance expertise and make candidates highly attractive to employers looking to implement AI solutions at scale.

Ultimately, software engineering and IT professionals who embrace AI will thrive in an industry that's evolving faster than ever. Whether it's writing cleaner, more efficient code, securing enterprise networks, or automating cloud infrastructure, AI is redefining how tech professionals work. By upskilling with AI certifications and hands-on experience, engineers and IT specialists can position themselves as indispensable assets in the rapidly shifting tech landscape. Staying ahead isn't just about keeping up with AI—it's about learning how to make AI work for you.

5.5 AI TOOLS FOR HUMAN RESOURCES & RECRUITING

For professionals in human resources and recruiting, AI has revolutionized how talent is sourced, screened, and retained. In 2025, AI-powered applicant tracking systems (ATS) like HireVue, Workday, and Greenhouse can automatically rank candidates based on job descriptions, past experience, and even soft skills using natural language processing (NLP). Recruiters no longer have to sift through hundreds of resumes manually—AI speeds up the process while reducing bias by focusing purely on qualifications. Additionally, AI-driven chatbots can handle initial candidate inquiries, schedule interviews, and even conduct pre-screening assessments, freeing up HR professionals to focus on high-value decision-making and relationship-building.

To stay ahead in the evolving HR landscape, professionals should upskill with AI-focused HR certifications. Some of the top options in 2025 include the AIHR (Academy to Innovate HR) Artificial Intelligence for HR Certification, SHRM People Analytics Specialty Credential, and the LinkedIn Learning AI in Recruiting Certificate. These certifications help HR professionals understand AI-driven hiring trends, optimize workforce analytics, and implement AI in an ethical way when it comes to talent management. Mastering these tools not only makes recruiters more efficient but also ensures they stay competitive in a rapidly evolving job market.

As AI continues to reshape HR and recruiting, those who embrace it will thrive in the field. AI tools can analyze employee sentiment and even predict potential turnover risks. However, the human element remains critical—AI can provide insights, but it's up to HR professionals to make the final call and foster genuine connections with candidates who are the right fit for the job. By learning how to leverage AI effectively, HR specialists can become more strategic, data-driven, and indispensable inside their organizations.

5.6 AI TOOLS FOR LEGAL WORK & COMPLIANCE

For legal professionals and compliance officers, AI has become a game-changer, streamlining research, contract review, and regulatory compliance. In 2025, AI-powered tools like Harvey AI, Casetext, and LexisNexis AI can analyze massive amounts of case law, contracts, and regulations in seconds—what used to take hours of manual research now takes minutes. AI-powered contract analysis tools can flag potential risks, inconsistencies, or missing clauses, ensuring airtight agreements. Compliance professionals, particularly those in finance, healthcare, and corporate governance, can also leverage AI for real-time risk detection, keeping their organizations ahead of shifting regulations.

To stay competitive, legal professionals should upskill with AI-driven legal and compliance certifications. The MIT AI for Legal Professionals Certificate, the Certified Information Privacy Professional (CIPP-AI), and the Harvard AI in Law & Ethics Program are excellent options. These certifications equip professionals with the knowledge to integrate AI into legal workflows, understand AI's ethical implications in law, and enhance compliance automation. By mastering AI-powered legal research, contract automation, and regulatory monitoring, lawyers and compliance officers can work more efficiently while reducing errors and legal risks.

While AI is revolutionizing legal work, it won't replace critical thinking, negotiation, and strategic decision-making—skills that only experienced legal professionals can provide. AI can summarize case law, draft legal documents, and analyze trends, but lawyers and compliance officers still need to interpret and apply that information with human judgment and expertise that is only learned from their education and experience on the job. Those who embrace AI will future-proof their careers, making themselves indispensable as firms and corporations increasingly adopt AI-driven legal tech to cut costs, improve accuracy, and enhance productivity.

5.7 AI TOOLS FOR EDUCATION & E-LEARNING

For teachers and e-learning educators, AI is transforming the way lessons are created, delivered, and personalized. In 2025, AI-powered platforms like ChatGPT, Khanmigo, and Coursera AI will allow educators to automate lesson planning, generate interactive quizzes, and even provide real-time feedback on student performance. AI-driven learning analytics help teachers identify struggling students earlier, allowing them to tailor lesson plans to individual needs. With AI chatbots handling routine questions and grading, educators can spend more time fostering critical thinking, creativity, and deeper discussions in their classrooms.

To stay ahead in the AI-driven education landscape, educators can pursue certifications that demonstrate expertise in AI-enhanced teaching methods. Programs like the ISTE Certified Educator in AI & EdTech, the Google AI for Educators Certification, and the Microsoft Certified Educator (MCE) in AI for Learning equip teachers with skills in adaptive learning technologies, AI-driven curriculum design, and digital classroom management. These credentials boost career prospects and ensure that educators can effectively integrate AI tools into their teaching strategies to improve student engagement and retention.

While AI can streamline administrative tasks and personalize learning, the role of educators remains irreplaceable. AI can generate resources, but teachers provide genuine human connection, mentorship, and emotional intelligence that technology cannot replicate.

Those who embrace AI will future-proof their careers by becoming leaders in AI-driven education, helping students absorb knowledge and develop the critical thinking skills needed in an increasingly automated world.

5.8 AI TOOLS FOR RETAIL & E-COMMERCE

In the fast-moving world of retail and e-commerce, AI has become a game-changer for everything from customer insights to inventory management. AI-powered tools like Shopify Magic, Amazon Personalize, and Google AI for Retail allow professionals to analyze shopping behaviors, predict demand, and make personalized recommendations in ways that were once thought impossible. With AI-driven chatbots handling customer service inquiries 24/7, and automated pricing tools adjusting costs in real-time based on market trends, retail and e-commerce workers who leverage AI can stay ahead of consumer expectations while optimizing efficiency. Whether you're managing an online store, overseeing supply chains, or crafting product descriptions, AI is reshaping the way retail operates in 2025.

To enhance AI expertise in retail and e-commerce, professionals can earn certifications that highlight their skills in AI-powered business strategies. Certifications like the IBM AI for Business Certification, Google Advanced Data Analytics Professional Certificate, and MIT's AI in Retail & Marketing course teach everything from AI-driven marketing automation to predictive inventory control. Listing these certifications on a resume signals to employers and clients that you are fluent in AI-driven commerce and ready to adapt to changing consumer trends. Learning how to implement AI-powered product recommendations, fraud detection systems, and chatbot automation can help professionals streamline operations and boost sales.

While AI can optimize pricing strategies, automate customer interactions, and personalize the shopping experience, human expertise remains essential for understanding brand voice, managing vendor relationships, and making strategic decisions. Retail professionals who embrace AI will not only increase productivity and customer satisfaction but also future-proof their careers in an industry that thrives on innovation. Those who integrate AI into their daily workflows will position themselves as leaders in the next era of retail and e-commerce.

5.9 AI TOOLS FOR MANUFACTURING & SUPPLY CHAIN MANAGEMENT

AI is revolutionizing manufacturing and supply chain management, making processes smarter, faster, and more efficient. From predictive maintenance in factories to AI-driven demand forecasting, professionals in this field are seeing firsthand how automation and data analytics can reduce costs and improve efficiency. AI-powered tools like Siemens MindSphere, IBM Watson Supply Chain, and SAP AI-driven logistics help track shipments in real-time and predict supply chain disruptions before they happen while optimizing inventory management to minimize waste and maximize profits. Those who embrace AI in manufacturing and supply chains are positioning themselves as indispensable experts in an industry that thrives on precision and efficiency.

For professionals looking to boost their AI expertise, several certifications can give them an edge in the job market. Earning credentials like the MIT Supply Chain Analytics Certificate, the APICS Certified Supply Chain Professional (CSCP) with AI coursework, and the Microsoft AI-900 (AI Fundamentals) certification can demonstrate expertise in AI-driven logistics, machine learning for inventory forecasting, and automation in warehouse management. These certifications show employers that you're not just keeping up—you're staying ahead by integrating cutting-edge AI solutions into the supply chain. Adding these to a resume signals that you understand how AI can eliminate inefficiencies, reduce downtime, and improve overall production quality.

While AI can predict demand shifts, automate procurement, and streamline production lines, human expertise is still essential for strategic decision-making, crisis management, and quality control. The future of manufacturing and supply chain management will be a blend of human intuition and AI-powered efficiency. Those who leverage AI tools instead of fearing them will increase productivity and job security while setting themselves up as industry leaders in a rapidly evolving landscape.

5.10 AI TOOLS FOR INSIDE SALES, CUSTOMER SERVICE & SUPPORT

AI is reshaping the world of inside sales, customer service, and support, making it easier than ever for professionals to connect with customers, close deals, and provide exceptional service. AI-powered tools like chatbots, virtual assistants, and sentiment analysis software allow sales reps and customer service agents to respond faster, anticipate customer needs, and personalize interactions like never before. With AI-driven customer relationship management (CRM) platforms like Salesforce Einstein, HubSpot AI, and Zoho AI, professionals can automate follow-ups, analyze customer behavior, and even get real-time coaching on how to handle objections or close deals. Those who embrace AI in these roles won't just keep up with industry changes—they'll set the new standard for customer engagement.

For professionals looking to level up their AI skills, there are several valuable certifications that can boost their expertise and impress potential employers. Earning credentials like the HubSpot Sales Software Certification, the Salesforce AI Associate Certification, or the Google AI for Business Certificate can demonstrate a profound understanding of AI-driven sales forecasting, automated customer interactions, and lead prioritization. These certifications highlight that you know how to use AI tools to optimize workflows, increase conversion rates, and improve customer satisfaction. Listing them on a resume tells employers that you're ahead of the curve, ready to leverage AI for better sales and support outcomes.

While AI can analyze data, recommend responses, and automate routine tasks, human intuition is still the most important factor in building relationships and closing deals. AI isn't here to replace inside sales and customer service professionals—it's here to enhance their abilities by freeing them up from repetitive tasks so they can focus on the real game-changer: fostering a real human connection that leaves the customer with a sense of relief at the end of each interaction that your company is always there and will always continue to have their back, no matter what.

5.11 AI TOOLS FOR DIGITAL CONTENT CREATORS

For digital content creators navigating platforms like Instagram Reels, TikTok, Snapchat, YouTube, and Facebook Stories, AI is an absolute game-changer. AI-powered tools can automate video editing, generate captions, suggest trending topics, and even analyze audience engagement in real-time. Apps like Adobe Sensei, CapCut, Runway ML, and Kapwing use AI to enhance video quality, remove backgrounds, and add dynamic effects—no advanced editing skills are required. AI-driven analytics tools like TubeBuddy and VidIQ help YouTubers understand which keywords, hashtags, and posting times will maximize engagement, while TikTok's built-in AI recommends optimal song choices, filters, and content trends to help videos go viral. By leveraging these tools, creators can work smarter, not harder—producing high-quality, attention-grabbing content faster than ever.

For those looking to legitimize their AI expertise and stand out in a crowded digital landscape, earning AI-focused certifications can provide a major boost. Platforms like Google, Meta, and HubSpot offer courses on AI-driven marketing, content strategy, and analytics. The Google AI for Creators Certification, the Meta Certified Digital Marketing Associate, and the YouTube Creator Academy's AI & Analytics Course are all excellent options for learning how to harness AI for video optimization, audience targeting, and social media growth. Listing these certifications on a resume or in a media kit tells brands and potential collaborators that you're not just creating content—you're strategically using AI to make it more effective and engaging.

The most successful content creators in 2025 aren't just good at filming and editing—they're AI-savvy digital strategists who know how to hack the algorithm, analyze performance metrics, and automate the tedious parts of content creation. AI doesn't replace creativity—it enhances it, freeing up creators to focus on storytelling, brand building, and community engagement. Those who embrace AI tools and continuously adapt will stay ahead of trends, grow their platforms faster, and land more brand partnerships in an increasingly competitive space.

5.12 AI TOOLS FOR JOURNALISM & MEDIA

For journalists and media professionals, AI is rapidly transforming how stories are researched, written, and distributed. AI-powered tools like ChatGPT, Jasper, and Copy.ai can assist with drafting articles, generating headlines, and even summarizing lengthy reports—helping journalists work faster without sacrificing quality. Platforms like Google's Journalist Studio and Grammarly AI aid in fact-checking, grammar refinement, and tone adjustments, ensuring content is polished and professional. Meanwhile, AI-driven analytics tools such as Chartbeat and Parse.ly help media professionals track audience engagement, predict trending topics, and optimize article placement for maximum reach. By integrating AI into their workflow, journalists can spend less time on tedious tasks and more time on investigative reporting, storytelling, and breaking news coverage.

For those looking to future-proof their careers, earning AI-focused certifications in media and journalism can provide a competitive edge. Programs like the Google News Initiative's AI for Journalists, the Knight Center's AI in Journalism Course, and the Associated Press AI Ethics Training equip reporters with skills in automated content generation, data journalism, and ethical AI practices. Additionally, certifications in SEO and AI-driven content strategy from platforms like HubSpot and Coursera can help journalists stay ahead of the game in a media landscape where AI-powered search engines and content recommendation algorithms shape audience engagement. Listing these certifications on a résumé signals to employers that you're not just a writer—you're an AI-savvy journalist who understands the future of digital news.

AI isn't here to replace journalists—it's here to enhance their ability to gather, analyze, and report the news with greater speed and accuracy. Reporters who embrace AI for research, content creation, and audience engagement will be best positioned to thrive in an industry that is evolving faster than ever. Whether it's using AI for transcribing interviews, generating data visualizations, or even personalizing news content for different audiences, those who adapt will remain indispensable in the ever-changing world of journalism and media.

AI is making waves in content creation, from writing to storytelling. AI writing assistants enhance content quality by suggesting edits, improving grammar, and even offering creativity prompts. Scriptwriting tools powered by AI are generating movie scripts, helping writers brainstorm ideas and structure their narratives. Imagine an AI program that knows all the tropes and plot twists, guiding you to craft a blockbuster screenplay. It's not about replacing writers; it's about giving them a digital quill that never runs out of ink.

While AI is enhancing productivity across industries, the most adaptable professionals will be those who learn how to leverage AI tools effectively. Whether it's mastering AI automation, analytics, or predictive modeling, upskilling is key to staying competitive in an AI-driven job market.

5.13 AI'S IMPACT ON THE SKILLED TRADES

The skilled trades industry has long been rooted in hands-on expertise, craftsmanship, and real-world problem-solving from someone who is physically present, making it basically impossible to replace with AI. But in recent years, AI has made its way into the trades, enhancing efficiency, safety, and precision in ways that were once thought unimaginable. From AI-driven predictive maintenance in HVAC systems to robot-assisted welding in manufacturing, technology is reshaping the landscape of skilled labor. Electricians, plumbers, machinists, and construction workers are now leveraging AI-powered tools that can diagnose issues faster, automate repetitive tasks, and improve accuracy in measurements and installations. While these advancements don't replace human skills, they do streamline workflows and create new opportunities for workers who embrace AI as part of their toolkit.

For those in the trades looking to stay ahead, AI-focused certifications can be a game-changer. Programs like the National Institute for Metalworking Skills (NIMS) Smart Manufacturing Certification, Autodesk's AI-driven CAD training, and AI-enhanced predictive maintenance courses are helping trade professionals integrate AI into their skill sets. Electricians can use AI for energy efficiency diagnostics, mechanics can train in AI-powered vehicle diagnostics, and builders can take advantage of machine learning software to optimize project planning. Having these certifications listed on a résumé not only sets workers apart in a competitive job market but also signals to employers that they're ready to adapt to the future of skilled labor.

The trades will always require human expertise, but those who embrace AI will have a significant advantage. As AI-powered tools become more accessible, skilled workers who learn to use them will work faster, reduce errors, and stay competitive in an evolving industry. Whether it's automating routine inspections, improving precision in fabrication, or enhancing job site safety, AI is proving to be a valuable partner in the skilled trades.

Key Takeaways from Chapter 5:

- **AI is transforming every industry** – Whether you're an accountant, marketer, educator, or tradesperson, AI-powered tools are enhancing efficiency, automating tedious tasks, and allowing professionals to focus on more strategic, high-value work. Those who learn to work alongside AI will have a distinct advantage in their field.
- **Upskilling with AI-focused certifications is a game-changer** – Many industries now offer AI-related certifications that demonstrate proficiency in AI tools and automation. Earning credentials like the AI in Accounting and Finance Certificate, Google AI for Business, or AI-powered HR certifications can help professionals stand out in the job market and future-proof their careers.
- **AI doesn't replace human expertise—it amplifies it** – While AI can automate repetitive tasks and generate insights, human judgment, creativity, and decision-making remain irreplaceable. The most successful professionals will be those who use AI as a tool to enhance their problem-solving abilities, not as a crutch to replace critical thinking.
- **The skilled trades industry is evolving with AI, too** – While hands-on work like plumbing, construction, and

electrical work can't be fully automated, AI-powered diagnostics, predictive maintenance, and digital modeling tools are helping tradespeople work smarter and more efficiently. Those who adapt AI into their workflows will stay ahead in a field that remains in high demand.

- **AI literacy is becoming a necessary skill for career growth** – Just like learning to use computers once they became essential in the modern workplace, understanding AI will soon be a fundamental requirement across industries. Professionals who invest time in learning AI tools, automation software, and data-driven decision-making will be the ones best positioned for success.

The future of work is changing, and AI is at the center of this transformation. But instead of fearing automation, professionals should see it as an opportunity to level up, become more efficient, and take their careers to new heights. By embracing AI tools, earning industry-specific certifications, and staying ahead of technological trends, you can ensure that you're not just keeping up—you're leading the charge. The key to long-term success isn't resisting change—it's leveraging AI to work smarter, build better, and future-proof a career that will always be in demand.

Now that we've covered AI's impact in the workplace, it's time to explore how AI can boost your resume, assist in job searches, and even make life easier at the office.

Bonus: A ChatGPT Prompt to Know More About AI Certifications Related to a Career Field

Prompt: "I work in [your industry or job role], and I want to learn more about AI to stay competitive in my field. Can you recommend some relevant AI certifications that will help me level up in my career? Please include options for beginners as well as advanced professionals, and note whether they are free or paid."

This prompt works well because it tells ChatGPT exactly what the person does and what they're looking for, making the response more tailored and useful. If they have a specific skill or goal in mind, they can add even more detail, like:

"I'm a digital marketer looking to learn about AI-driven analytics and automation. What AI certifications would be most valuable for me?"

6

USING AI TO BOOST YOUR RESUME, ASSIST IN JOB SEARCHES, AND ENHANCE YOUR CAREER

A 2023-24 IBM study, which gathered insights from 3,000 business executives from 30+ countries and 26 different industries worldwide about generative AI, revealed some compelling statistics: 75% of those surveyed believe that AI would provide their companies with a competitive advantage, while 43% are already leveraging AI to inform strategic decisions.

In the IBM study, Kazuhiro Nishiyama, President of Kansai Mirai Bank, Limited, had a particular quote about artificial intelligence that really stood out: "As AI develops, there will be three types of people: those who create AI, those who use AI, and those who are used by AI." Which one are you?

In another revealing 2023 survey conducted by Fishbowl, a platform for workplace discussions, over 11,700 employees from leading companies like Amazon, Google, Meta, and Twitter (now X) were asked about their use of AI in the workplace. Interestingly, 43% of these respondents acknowledged utilizing AI tools to facilitate their job tasks. Yet, 68% of this group admitted to not informing their supervisors about their use of these AI solutions.

We are already seeing AI, and it's large impact in workplaces across the world, but the real question is this: how do you harness its power in ways that apply to you in your career?

6.1 AI IN HUMAN RESOURCES & RECRUITING: ADAPTING TO AN EVER-CHANGING GAME

As previously mentioned in Chapter 5, Section 5, the continued growth of AI being used in recruitment and job postings, means that we all must adapt our strategies when it comes to searching for that next job or promotion.

The advent of AI has transformed the landscape of how recruiters and human resources departments find, evaluate, and keep talent. By the year 2025, AI-enhanced applicant tracking systems (ATS) such as HireVue, Workday, and Greenhouse are equipped to autonomously evaluate candidates against job requirements, their prior roles, and even their soft skills through the use of natural language processing (NLP).

This innovation means recruiters can bypass the time-consuming task of manually reviewing countless resumes, but it also means that not having the right keywords in a resume or cover letter for a job posting could mean that your application is blocked by AI before a human ever gets real eyes on it. In this chapter, we'll break down exactly how you can use AI to enhance your job applications, stand out in a crowded market, and land the opportunities you deserve.

6.2 AI IN JOB HUNTING: SMARTER WAYS TO SEARCH AND APPLY

Job hunting in today's competitive market can feel like a full-time job in itself. Crafting the perfect resume, tweaking it for each position, and writing personalized cover letters can take hours—sometimes days. But thanks to AI, tools like ChatGPT are making the process easier, faster, and far more efficient. Instead of manually reworking your resume by hand for each job posting, AI can quickly tailor your application to match the keywords and qualifications listed in each job description. This means you're not just applying to more jobs in less time—you're increasing your chances of actually getting noticed by recruiters and applicant tracking systems (ATS).

Why is this important? One of the biggest advantages of using AI for job searching is its ability to optimize your resume for different industries and roles. Many companies use ATS software to scan and filter resumes before a human ever sees them, and if yours doesn't include the right keywords, it might never make it past the first round and find its way to the shred bin.

ChatGPT can analyze a job listing and suggest improvements to your resume, ensuring it highlights the exact skills, experience, and terminology that hiring managers are looking for. It can also help generate a compelling cover letter, saving you the hassle of starting from scratch for every application. With AI streamlining these steps, you can focus on networking, interview prep, and other job search strategies that require a human touch. This can also save you precious time. Instead of having to completely redo your entire resume by hand to suit the needs of every job listing you're interested in, let ChatGPT do some of the heavy lifting.

Beyond just resumes and cover letters, AI can also assist with other crucial aspects of job searching. Need a LinkedIn profile update? ChatGPT can help refine your summary, suggest strong headlines, and even craft engaging posts to showcase your expertise. Struggling with interview preparation? AI can simulate common interview questions and help you refine your responses. Whether you're switching careers, re-entering the workforce, or just looking for better opportunities, AI-powered job search tools give you a competitive edge.

AI's benefits don't stop once you've landed an interview. ChatGPT can simulate interview scenarios, generate common interview questions, and even help you craft well-structured responses. By practicing with AI, jobseekers can refine their answers, build confidence, and prepare for tricky behavioral questions using structured response methods like STAR (Situation, Task, Action, Result). In a world where job competition is fierce, using AI as a job-search assistant isn't just a smart strategy—it's becoming a necessity. Whether you need help identifying job openings, optimizing your resume, or preparing for an interview, AI can be the ultimate tool to give you a competitive edge and land the job you want.

6.3 AI IN WORK PRODUCTIVITY: STREAMLINING YOUR DAY-TO-DAY TASKS

Imagine your day starting with an AI-powered assistant organizing your tasks as if a tiny digital butler lives in your phone. AI-powered task management tools are revolutionizing our productivity, transforming our chaotic "to-do" lists into streamlined, manageable plans. Smart scheduling is at the core, where AI-assisted calendar management takes the guesswork out of planning. It analyzes your tasks, priorities, and even your energy levels throughout the day to suggest the best times for meetings, deep work, and lunch breaks.

Time management is another realm where AI shines. Time tracking software analyzes your productivity patterns, revealing when you're at your peak and when you're likely to be distracted by—you know—those darn Instagram memes again. With this insight, you can allocate your time more efficiently, ensuring that you work when you're most productive and still take breaks when you need them. Focus-enhancing applications are also in the mix, minimizing distractions by gently nudging you back on track when your attention starts to wander.

And if you've ever spent more time searching for a document than actually working on it, AI in information retrieval is your new best friend. Intelligent search engines provide contextual search results, understanding not just what you're looking for but why. Document summarization is another nifty feature, offering AI-generated content overviews that help you grasp the essence of lengthy reports without reading every single word. Imagine reading the cliff notes of a novel but for your work documents, allowing you to stay informed without getting bogged down.

Incorporating AI into productivity tools transforms the way we work. These technologies not only enhance efficiency but also bring a sense of ease and balance to our daily routines. By automating repetitive tasks and optimizing our schedules, AI allows us to focus on what truly matters, whether it's a creative project or simply enjoying a cup of coffee without the nagging thought of an overflowing inbox. The possibilities are endless, and as AI evolves, we can expect even smarter, more intuitive tools to make our lives easier.

6.4 USING AI TO BOOST EFFICIENCY AT THE OFFICE

For those working in an office environment, staying organized and productive can often feel like a full-time job in itself. Between managing emails, attending meetings, juggling deadlines, and handling daily tasks, it's easy to get overwhelmed. That's where specific AI tools come in—not just as job search assistants but as powerful productivity boosters. Trello with Butler AI can help streamline workflows, automate repetitive tasks, and provide valuable insights that allow office professionals to focus on what really matters. Whether it's optimizing a schedule, summarizing key points from meetings, or even drafting emails, AI can be your virtual assistant that enhances efficiency and keeps you on top of your responsibilities.

One of the biggest benefits of using AI in the workplace is email management. Sorting through an overflowing inbox can be a major time drain, but an AI tool like Superhuman can help you organize your inbox better, automate responses, and even speed up inbox processing, allowing you to move on to more critical tasks. Additionally, AI tools can help prioritize incoming emails, flagging urgent messages while filtering out less important ones, ensuring that high-priority items don't get buried under an avalanche of unread messages.

You can even create a simple productivity planner using ChatGPT. Ask for a template that includes sections for daily goals, appointments, and key tasks. Customize it with your personal touch, and use it to map out a more productive day.

There are even tools like Krisp AI, which is an AI-powered noise cancellation tool that removes background noise from virtual meetings.

Finally, let's not forget the importance of breaks. Even machines need downtime, and so do you. Smart Assistants like Siri, Google Assistant, or Alexa can even remind you to take regular breaks with prompts like: "Set a reminder to stretch and hydrate every hour." These small pauses can rejuvenate your mind, keeping you sharp and focused throughout the day. With AI's assistance, you'll find yourself navigating the tides of productivity with ease, turning hectic days into harmonious ones.

AI is also a game-changer when it comes to meeting organization and note-taking. Otter.ai and Fireflies.ai can automatically transcribe work meetings, interviews, and lectures in real time with AI-generated notes and summaries. If a team member misses a meeting, AI can provide a summary with important action items, eliminating the need to sift through an hour-long recording. This makes collaboration more efficient and ensures that everyone stays aligned on goals and responsibilities.

Beyond organization, AI can enhance productivity by automating repetitive office tasks. Whether it's generating reports, creating presentations, or analyzing data trends, AI tools can handle the heavy lifting, freeing up time for more strategic thinking. For professionals who need to quickly understand complex information, ChatGPT can summarize lengthy reports, research findings, and industry trends, making it easier to stay informed without dedicating hours to reading. By integrating AI into daily office routines, employees can work smarter, not harder—leading to greater efficiency, better time management, and ultimately, more job satisfaction.

6.5 ENHANCING SMALL BUSINESS OPERATIONS WITH AI

Picture this: you're running a bustling cafe, juggling everything from customer orders to inventory management, and wondering if maybe you should hire an octopus to help out. Enter AI, your digital octopus, ready to lend a hand in more ways than you might have imagined. For small businesses, AI isn't just a buzzword; it's a game changer. It provides tools that can simplify your operations, making you the maestro of your entrepreneurial orchestra. Take customer relationship management (CRM) systems like Salesforce, for example. These systems use AI to analyze customer data, predict needs, and personalize interactions. It's like having a psychic barista who knows what customers want before they even order. With AI-driven CRM, you can enhance customer loyalty and boost sales, all while sipping your morning espresso.

Inventory management is another area where AI flexes its muscles. Imagine having a tool that tracks stock levels in real time, predicts future demand, and even suggests optimal reorder points. AI-driven stock tracking ensures you never run out of your best-selling muffins or overstock those seasonal lattes. It's like having a crystal ball that helps you make informed decisions, keeping your shelves stocked and your customers happy. By optimizing your inventory management, you can reduce waste, save money, and improve operational efficiency, all without needing to consult an actual fortune-teller.

AI's magic extends into marketing and sales, transforming how small businesses attract and retain customers. Targeted advertising is one of AI's superpowers, allowing you to reach the right audience with the right message at the right time. Instead of casting a wide net and hoping for the best, AI helps you place ads where they're most likely to be seen by potential customers. Sales forecasting is another area where AI shines, using data to predict sales trends and guide inventory and staffing decisions. With AI, you can anticipate busy periods, adjust staffing levels, and even plan customer promotions to maximize revenue. It's like having a business partner who always knows when the next big rush is coming.

Operational efficiency is the backbone of any successful business, and AI offers the tools to streamline processes and boost productivity. Automated invoicing, for instance, speeds up billing cycles and reduces the chance of human error. No more late payments or misplaced invoices; AI ensures everything runs like clockwork. Resource allocation is another area where AI excels, optimizing staff schedules based on predicted demand. It's like having a scheduler who knows every employee's strengths and weaknesses, ensuring the right people are in the right place at the right time. By automating these tasks, you free up valuable time and resources, allowing you to focus on growing your business.

Now, implementing AI in your small business doesn't have to feel like moving a mountain. Start with gradual adoption, testing the waters with pilot projects before diving in headfirst. This approach allows you to experiment with AI tools and assess their impact on your operations. It's like sampling a new menu item before committing to a full rollout. Employee training is also crucial, ensuring your team is comfortable with new tools and processes. By involving your staff in the transition, you can build a culture of innovation and adaptability, making the integration of AI a seamless experience for everyone involved.

Incorporating AI into your small business is about more than just keeping up with the competition; it's about embracing a new way of working that enhances efficiency, improves customer satisfaction, and drives growth. If AI can make your coffee shop run smoother and your customers happier, imagine what it can do for the rest of your business. As we wrap up this chapter, consider the possibilities AI offers for your enterprise and how these tools can transform your operations for the better.

Key Takeaways from Chapter 6:

- **AI is Already Changing the Workplace** – A 2023-24 IBM study showed that 75% of business executives believe AI provides a competitive advantage, and nearly half are already using it for strategic decisions. As AI continues to evolve, learning how to leverage it in your career will be crucial.
- **AI-Powered Resume Optimization** – Many companies now use applicant tracking systems (ATS) to filter resumes before a human even sees them. AI tools like ChatGPT can help tailor your resume and cover letter with the right keywords and formatting, increasing your chances of passing these automated screenings.
- **Smarter Job Hunting with AI** – AI can accelerate the job search process by analyzing job descriptions, customizing applications, and even generating LinkedIn updates and networking messages. It can also assist with interview preparation by simulating common questions and structuring effective responses.
- **Smart Scheduling & Time Management** – AI tools analyze productivity patterns to suggest the best times for

meetings, deep work, and breaks, helping professionals stay efficient without burning out.

- **Focus & Distraction Reduction** – AI-driven time tracking and focus-enhancing applications keep distractions at bay, ensuring better concentration and workflow.
- **Work Smarter, Not Harder** – AI-powered automation frees up time for more important work, helping professionals reduce stress, boost efficiency, and maintain a better work-life balance.

Artificial intelligence is reshaping the job market, and those who learn how to use it effectively will have a major advantage. Whether you're searching for a new job, updating your resume, or looking to increase efficiency at the office, AI tools can help streamline these processes. From optimizing applications with the right keywords to automating daily workplace tasks, AI isn't just a luxury—it's becoming a necessity for staying competitive in the workforce. The future of work isn't about AI replacing people—it's about people who know how to use AI effectively leading the way.

In the next chapter, we'll dive into practical ways AI can help make life easier, more practical, and even more enjoyable outside of work.

Bonus: A ChatGPT Prompt for Rewriting A Resume to Match the Applicant Tracking System (ATS) Keywords in a Job Description

Prompt: "I am applying for a [job title] position at [company name], and I want to make sure my resume and cover letter are optimized for Applicant Tracking Systems (ATS). Here is the job description: [paste job description]. Can you help me rewrite my resume and cover letter using the right keywords and formatting so that it gets past the ATS and stands out to hiring managers?"

This prompt works well because it provides key details—the job title, company name, and job description—so ChatGPT can tailor the resume and cover letter with relevant keywords and phrasing that match the ATS filters.

For an extra edge, they can also ask ChatGPT:

"Can you analyze this job description and pull out the most important keywords and skills I should include in my resume to improve my chances of passing an ATS?"

This helps job seekers ensure they're aligning their skills and experience with exactly what the employer is looking for.

7
THE BENEFITS OF USING AI AT HOME

This chapter is dedicated to continuing your transformation into an AI-competent individual. Visualize AI as a personal toolkit filled with cutting-edge tools designed to keep you at the forefront. Acquiring the fundamentals of AI allows you to make well-informed decisions and leverage AI to your benefit. In today's world, where AI integration is everywhere, staying informed about these concepts ensures you're always prepared to face new challenges.

7.1 USING AI TO SET AND ACHIEVE GOALS

Imagine having a personal assistant who remembers your goals and nudges you toward them with the precision of a life coach. Platforms like Stride and Habitica use AI to assist in planning and prioritization, ensuring your goals aren't just dreams scribbled in a dusty journal. With progress tracking, AI analytics monitor your achievements, providing insights that help adjust your plans as needed, much like a fitness tracker that celebrates every step you take toward your health goals.

Habitica is a popular goal tracker because it can turn achieving personal goals into a role-playing game (RPG), while rewarding users for completing tasks, helping to maintain motivational levels by making one feel like as if they are leveling up in a game each time they make progress.

Creating positive habits can feel like trying to teach a cat to fetch, but AI is here to transform that challenge. Habit-tracking apps equipped with AI reminders and progress reports are like having a motivational speaker in your pocket, cheering you on. By analyzing your behavior, AI provides insights into patterns that might be sabotaging your efforts, offering suggestions to tweak your approach. With AI's support, forming good habits becomes less about discipline and more about harnessing technology to work smarter, not harder.

Personal growth is a journey, not a destination, and AI can be your compass. AI-driven personalized coaching offers tailored advice and motivation, acting as a mentor who knows your strengths and areas for improvement. Self-reflection tools powered by AI provide journaling and mindfulness exercises, helping you explore your thoughts and emotions with the ease of guided meditation. With AI, self-improvement becomes an engaging and enlightening experience, rather than feeling like a chore.

7.2 A SMARTER APPROACH TO HEALTH AND FITNESS WITH AI

Artificial intelligence isn't just transforming how we work—it's also revolutionizing how we take care of ourselves. Whether you're looking to eat healthier, become more active, or track your fitness progress, AI-powered tools can help make personal health management easier and more effective. From smartwatches that track workouts to AI-driven nutrition apps that suggest personalized meal plans, technology is making it possible to take control of your health from the comfort of your own home.

One of the most popular ways AI is helping people stay active is through smart fitness tracking devices. Wearable technology like the Apple Watch, Fitbit, and WHOOP use AI to monitor everything from step count and heart rate to sleep patterns and recovery times. These devices don't just track numbers; they analyze patterns and provide insights into how users can improve their fitness. AI-powered virtual coaches can even suggest personalized workout routines based on fitness levels and goals, ensuring that each workout is optimized for maximum effectiveness. Whether you're training for a marathon or just trying to get in 10,000 steps a day, AI can help keep you on track and motivated.

Beyond exercise, AI also plays a huge role in nutrition and meal planning. Apps like MyFitnessPal and Noom use AI to track food intake, analyze eating habits, and offer personalized diet recommendations. AI can scan barcodes on food packaging to provide instant nutritional breakdowns or suggest healthier alternatives based on dietary preferences. Some AI-driven meal-planning apps even generate grocery lists and suggest recipes based on what's available in the fridge, making it easier to eat well without the stress of figuring out what to cook. By leveraging AI for nutrition tracking, people can develop healthier eating habits and ensure they're fueling their bodies with the right nutrients.

Another key benefit of using AI for health and fitness is accountability and motivation. AI-powered apps and virtual assistants can send reminders to drink water, stretch, or go for a walk, ensuring that users stay consistent with their health goals. Some apps even use gamification techniques—rewarding users with badges, streaks, and progress charts—to keep them engaged and motivated. AI-based health assistants like Google Fit and Apple Health also integrate with other smart home devices, allowing users to set fitness goals and track progress effortlessly. With AI acting as a personal trainer, nutritionist, and accountability partner all in one, becoming healthier and more active has never been more accessible for all.

7.3 USING AI FOR MEAL PLANNING AND COOKING

Picture this: It's a weekday morning, and you're racing against the clock, your stomach growling louder than your alarm. You need something healthy, quick, and delicious to kickstart the day. Enter ChatGPT, your culinary sidekick, ready to whip up a breakfast recipe faster than you can say "sunny-side up." A simple prompt like, "Give me a healthy breakfast recipe that I can make in under 15 minutes," is all it takes. Suddenly, you're the proud chef of a vibrant smoothie packed with greens and fruits or perhaps a delightful bowl of overnight oats topped with berries. Maybe you want a quick egg scramble peppered with colorful veggies. These options satisfy your hunger and fuel your day, leaving you feeling like the superhero of your own morning routine.

Now, shift gears to dinnertime. You're committed to a plant-based diet, but the thought of planning the week's meals is as appealing as watching paint dry. Fear not! ChatGPT is here with a prompt like, "Suggest a week's worth of dinner ideas for someone following a plant-based diet." Suddenly, you're envisioning a menu that includes hearty lentil curries that warm the soul, tofu stir-fries bursting with flavor, and perhaps a creamy chickpea stew that even your carnivorous friends would envy. With ChatGPT's help, your meal planning transforms from a chore into a culinary adventure. No more staring blankly at an empty fridge while pondering what's for dinner. Instead, you're armed with a plan that excites your palate and honors your commitment to plant-based living.

If you want to be even more specific, you can alert ChatGPT to any food allergies that you have, as well as certain foods you don't like. This way, ChatGPT can whip up some even more specific recipes that aren't just time-saving and healthy, they are tailored towards your personal tastes. Remember, while this is a beginner's book, the more specific you are with ChatGPT, the more specific it will be with the solution. It can even learn your favorite food interests over time.

For those on a weight loss mission, you're not alone in this endeavor. A prompt such as, "What are some low-calorie meal options for weight loss that are easy to prepare?" opens the door to a world where flavor doesn't have to be sacrificed at the altar of calorie counting. Imagine digging into a zesty quinoa salad with a hint of lime or savoring a bowl of vegetable soup that's as comforting as it is nutritious. These meal ideas are not only easy to prepare but also designed to delight your taste buds while keeping your caloric intake in check.

Of course, if you're feeding a family of four on a budget, meal planning can sometimes feel like a tightrope walk between nutrition and cost. But here's ChatGPT to the rescue with a simple prompt: "What are some budget-friendly meal ideas for a family of four?" Suddenly, you're envisioning dinners that won't break the bank yet still offer a nutritious punch. Affordable ingredients transform into dishes like beef and vegetable stir-fry or comforting pasta bakes that warm the heart and soul. These meals are not only easy on the wallet but also bring the family together around the dinner table, fostering connections and creating memories. ChatGPT helps you plan meals that are as kind to your budget as they are to your family's well-being.

Using ChatGPT for meal planning simplifies the process, ensuring that you spend less time thinking about what to cook and more time enjoying delicious meals with family and friends. With ChatGPT and AI, every meal is an opportunity to savor, explore, and nourish, all while keeping your busy schedule in mind.

7.4 USING AI TO LEARN A NEW LANGUAGE QUICKER THAN EVER BEFORE

Learning a new language has traditionally been a time-consuming process, requiring textbooks, classes, and hours of memorization. But thanks to artificial intelligence, mastering a new language has never been more accessible or efficient. AI-powered language tools can provide real-time feedback, personalized lessons, and interactive exercises that adapt to each learner's progress. Whether you're preparing for an international trip, looking to advance in your career, or simply interested in expanding your linguistic skills, AI can fast-track the learning process in ways that traditional methods never could.

One of the biggest advantages of using AI for language learning is personalization. AI-driven platforms like Duolingo, Rosetta Stone, and Babbel use machine learning algorithms to analyze how a user learns best and then tailor lessons accordingly. These platforms adjust difficulty levels based on your strengths and weaknesses, ensuring that you focus on areas where you need improvement rather than repeating concepts you've already mastered. ChatGPT can also be an excellent resource, offering explanations of grammar rules, generating practice exercises, or even translating difficult phrases into simpler terms to aid comprehension.

Another game-changing feature of AI is its ability to provide instant, real-time feedback. AI-powered chatbots, such as ChatGPT, can simulate conversations in different languages, allowing users to practice speaking and writing with an interactive partner. Unlike traditional methods that rely on scheduled tutoring sessions, AI tools are available 24/7, making it easy to practice at any time. Many AI language tools also incorporate speech recognition, allowing users to improve their pronunciation by receiving immediate corrections. This eliminates the fear of making mistakes in front of others and creates a stress-free learning environment.

Beyond just structured lessons, AI enhances immersion, which is one of the best ways to learn a language quickly. AI-powered translation apps, such as Google Translate and DeepL, allow users to read foreign texts, understand menus, and even translate spoken conversations in real-time. AI-generated subtitles on streaming platforms help learners absorb vocabulary in a natural context while watching movies or shows in their target language. Whether you're chatting with an AI language tutor, practicing pronunciation, or translating everyday conversations, AI is revolutionizing the way people learn new languages—making it faster, more personalized, and more engaging than ever before.

7.5 HOW AI IS MAKING HOME IMPROVEMENT AND RENOVATIONS EASIER

Home renovation projects have always been a challenge, requiring careful planning, budgeting, and decision-making. In 2025, however, artificial intelligence has transformed the process, making it easier than ever for homeowners to visualize their ideas, estimate costs, and find the right professionals for the job. AI-powered tools can assist in every phase of a renovation, from generating design inspiration to comparing contractor qualifications. Whether someone is redesigning a single room or tackling a full-scale remodel, AI can help streamline the process and eliminate much of the guesswork. These tools are making home improvement more accessible while helping homeowners make more informed decisions: saving time and money.

One of the most exciting ways AI is assisting homeowners is through AI-powered design visualization tools. Apps like Remodel AI, RE Imagine Home, and Room AI allow users to upload photos of their space and test different design styles, color palettes, and furniture arrangements. Instead of relying on imagination alone, homeowners can see digital mockups of how their space might look before making any commitments. These tools help individuals clarify their preferences and communicate their ideas more effectively to contractors, reducing misunderstandings and costly mistakes. Although these AI-generated images are not perfect blueprints, they significantly speed up the design process by giving users a starting point and a clearer vision for their renovations.

Beyond design, AI is also making a major impact on budgeting and project planning. Renovation costs can vary widely based on location, materials, and labor availability, making it difficult to estimate a realistic budget. AI tools like ChatGPT and Renotag help homeowners generate cost estimates based on current market rates, giving them a clearer picture of what their project might cost before reaching out to contractors. These tools analyze factors such as material expenses, labor costs, and time requirements, helping homeowners avoid financial surprises. While AI-generated estimates still require confirmation from professionals, they serve as a useful starting point, allowing homeowners to plan more effectively and compare pricing before committing to a project.

Finding and hiring the right contractor is another crucial step in the renovation process, and AI is making this task easier as well. AI-powered chatbots can quickly scan local contractor reviews, check certifications, and help homeowners determine the specific type of professional they need for their projects. Rather than spending hours researching different contractors manually, homeowners can use AI to generate a shortlist of qualified professionals in their area. Additionally, many contractor websites now feature AI chatbots that can answer initial questions about services, pricing, and availability. While AI can simplify the search process, it's still essential for homeowners to verify information, read multiple reviews, and get estimates from at least three different professionals before making a final decision.

Overall, AI has made home improvement projects more manageable, helping homeowners visualize designs, estimate budgets, and find qualified contractors with ease. These tools reduce the stress and uncertainty that often accompany renovations, allowing homeowners to focus on bringing their vision to life. While AI should not replace expert human input, it serves as an incredibly valuable assistant, guiding homeowners through the process with greater confidence and efficiency. As AI technology continues to evolve, the home renovation industry is becoming more accessible and streamlined, ensuring that even the most ambitious projects can be tackled with the help of smart, AI-driven solutions.

7.6 USING AI FOR PERSONAL FINANCE

AI is revolutionizing personal finance by offering tools that automate budgeting, provide personalized financial advice, and enhance overall money management. These AI-driven applications analyze spending patterns, track expenses, and suggest tailored strategies to help individuals achieve their financial goals. By leveraging machine learning algorithms, these tools offer real-time insights and predictive analytics, making financial planning more accessible and efficient.

Here are some advantages of AI-powered budgeting tools:

- **Automated Expense Tracking:** AI tools automatically monitor and categorize expenditures, eliminating the need for manual entry and reducing errors.
- **Personalized Budget Recommendations:** By analyzing individual spending habits, AI provides customized budgeting advice, helping users allocate funds more effectively.
- **Predictive Financial Planning:** AI utilizes predictive analytics to forecast future expenses and income, enabling proactive financial decision-making.

Here are some examples of AI-Driven Budgeting Tools:

- **Wally:** An AI-powered app that tracks spending, cash flow, and offers personalized financial advice.
- **Cleo:** A chatbot providing real-time insights into expenses, budgeting assistance, and financial tips.

- **Rocket Money:** An application that monitors recurring payments, identifies unnecessary expenses, and assists users in saving money through its Smart Savings feature.
- **Trim:** Analyzes spending habits, negotiates bills and cancels unwanted subscriptions to optimize savings.
- **QuickBooks:** Incorporates AI for cash flow forecasting and report generation, beneficial for small business owners.

To begin utilizing AI for budgeting, individuals can select a tool that aligns with their financial objectives and preferences. After connecting their financial accounts, the AI system will analyze transactions, categorize expenses, and provide insights. Users receive personalized recommendations and can set specific goals, such as saving for a vacation or reducing debt. Over time, the AI adapts to changes in spending behavior, ensuring that the advice remains relevant and effective.

Incorporating AI into personal finance simplifies the budgeting process and empowers individuals to make informed decisions, leading to improved financial well-being.

Key Takeaways from Chapter 7:

- **AI helps you set and achieve personal goals** – From habit tracking to AI-driven coaching, these tools help to keep you on track and stay motivated.
- **AI-powered fitness and health tools make staying active easier** – Smart wearables and AI-driven nutrition apps help personalize workouts and diet plans.
- **AI enhances home improvement projects** – Design visualization tools, cost estimators, and AI-powered contractor searches simplify renovations.
- **AI simplifies personal finance management** – Budgeting tools track expenses, provide spending insights and help users make smarter financial decisions.

- **AI accelerates learning and skill development** – Language-learning apps and educational tools use AI to personalize lessons and provide real-time feedback.
- **AI is a powerful assistant for everyday life** – From productivity hacks to better financial planning, AI is making daily tasks faster, smarter, and more efficient.

AI is no longer just a futuristic concept—it's a practical tool that is reshaping how we go about our everyday lives. Whether it's helping us set and achieve goals, stay on top of our health and fitness, learn new skills, renovate our homes, or manage our finances, AI-powered tools are making life easier, more efficient, and even more enjoyable. By embracing these technologies, we can automate tedious tasks, make more informed decisions, and free up valuable time to focus on what truly matters.

Bonus: A ChatGPT Prompt for a Personalized Workout Plan

Prompt: "I am a 45-year-old male, 5-foot-11, 225 lbs., and I want to lose 30 lbs. over the next four months. Can you create a 5-day per week workout regimen that balances strength training and cardio to help me achieve my goal? I also need recommendations on rest days, nutrition tips, and any AI-driven fitness tools or apps that can help track my progress."

This prompt works well because it gives ChatGPT key details about age, height, weight, goals, and time frame—allowing for a structured, goal-oriented fitness plan.

For additional guidance, they might also ask:

"Can you adjust the workout plan for someone with knee issues who needs lower-impact cardio options?"

OR

"Can you suggest AI-powered fitness apps or smartwatches that will track my progress and optimize my workouts in real time?"

This would enhance the AI-generated plan by incorporating wearable tech and smart tracking tools to keep them accountable.

8

ETHICAL AND SOCIETAL IMPLICATIONS AROUND AI

Up to this point, we've explored the essentials of AI and its impact on our individual lives. However, we have yet to delve into the future prospects of AI, its implications for society in the years ahead, and the potential challenges that come with adopting advanced AI technologies into our daily routines. It's important to navigate this emerging landscape in a manner that aligns with your personal beliefs and values, and to decide on what is best for you going forward.

8.1 DESIGNING ETHICAL AI SYSTEMS: PRINCIPLES AND PRACTICES

Imagine a world where AI is not just smart but also plays fair, like a referee who gets every call right. That's the dream, right? Fairness in AI means ensuring that outcomes are unbiased. This involves designing systems that treat all users equally, regardless of their background or demographic. Transparency is another cornerstone—making sure AI processes are as clear as a crystal ball. Users should understand how decisions are made, just like knowing why your GPS decided to take you on the scenic route to the grocery store. When AI systems are transparent, they become more accountable, enabling users and developers to trust them.

Of course, making AI ethical is as easy as teaching a cat to fetch. Bias in training data is a major hurdle. AI learns from data, and if that data is skewed, the AI becomes as biased as a picky eater. Addressing these disparities involves curating diverse datasets, ensuring they reflect the real world. Then there's accountability—assigning responsibility for AI decisions, so there's someone to call when things go awry instead of just shouting at your laptop. Developers and companies must step up to the plate, owning the outcomes of their AI systems along the way.

To create an ethical AI, we must embrace an inclusive design process. By involving diverse stakeholders from all walks of life, AI projects gain perspectives that prevent blind spots. It's like assembling a superhero team with varied powers, ensuring all bases are covered. Continuous evaluation of AI impacts is crucial, too. Regular assessments ensure systems remain aligned with ethical standards, adapting as needed. This ongoing vigilance helps maintain AI's integrity, just like regular check-ups keep your car running smoothly.

Ethical AI in practice is inspiring. In healthcare, AI systems are designed with patient privacy and informed consent at the forefront. This ensures information remains confidential, keeping trust intact. In finance, AI tools combat discrimination in credit scoring, assessing applicants fairly based on their merits. These systems are like a fair judge, ensuring everyone gets a fair shot at the opportunities presented to them.

8.2 HOW AI IS MAKING LIFE EASIER FOR PEOPLE WITH DISABILITIES

Artificial intelligence is revolutionizing accessibility, making daily life more manageable for individuals with physical and mental disabilities. From voice-activated assistants to real-time language translation, AI-powered tools are breaking down barriers that once made tasks like communication, mobility, and learning significantly more challenging. These advancements are not just about convenience—they're about empowering people to live more independently, engage with the world around them, and access opportunities that might have been difficult or impossible in the past. AI is proving to be a powerful ally in creating a more inclusive society where technology adapts to human needs rather than the other way around.

For individuals with physical disabilities, AI-driven assistive technologies are transforming how they navigate their daily lives. We've already discussed voice-controlled smart home devices like Alexa and Google Assistant, which allow users to turn lights on, adjust the thermostat, or even unlock doors, but for people with physical disabilities, this is a game-changer. AI-powered mobility aids, such as self-driving wheelchairs and wearable exoskeletons, are giving people with limited mobility newfound freedom. Additionally, AI-driven prosthetics can now adapt to a person's movement in real-time, improving comfort and functionality. These innovations ensure that physical limitations no longer dictate a person's ability to live independently and comfortably.

AI is also making major strides in supporting individuals with mental disabilities and neurodiverse conditions as well. AI-powered apps can assist people with autism in elevating their communication skills, recognizing social cues, and developing routines that help with daily tasks. For those with cognitive disabilities, AI-driven reminders and task-management tools help keep schedules on track, improve organization, and reduce anxiety in the process. In the realm of mental health, AI chatbots like Woebot and Wysa provide round-the-clock emotional support, offering coping strategies and guidance for managing stress, anxiety, and depression. These AI tools serve as a valuable supplement to professional care, ensuring people have constant access to support when they need it most.

Perhaps one of AI's most transformative impacts is in the area of communication and accessibility. Speech-to-text programs and AI-powered captioning services allow individuals who are deaf or hard of hearing to participate in conversations, meetings, and online content with greater ease. AI-driven text-to-speech applications help those with speech impairments communicate more effectively, giving them a voice in both personal and professional settings. For individuals with visual impairments, AI-powered screen readers like JAWS and voice assistants can describe digital content, translate images into spoken words, and even help navigate unfamiliar spaces using object recognition. As AI technology continues to evolve, it is improving accessibility and fostering greater inclusion, ensuring that no one is left behind in an increasingly digitalized world.

8.3 AI REGULATION AND POLICY: NAVIGATING THE LEGAL LANDSCAPE

Imagine trying to catch lightning in a bottle; that's what regulating AI feels like. Governments are scrambling to keep up with this fast-evolving tech landscape. The General Data Protection Regulation (GDPR) in Europe is a big player, focusing on data protection and user privacy. Countries are crafting national AI strategies, attempting to ride the tech wave while protecting citizens' rights in the process. These initiatives aim to create policies that encourage innovation but safeguard privacy, a bit like letting your kids play in the mud but insisting they wash up afterward.

However, regulating AI is like playing whack-a-mole; the moment you address one issue, another pops up. The rapid pace of AI development leaves lawmakers struggling to keep regulations current. And then there's the cross-border conundrum—how do you harmonize policies when AI knows no geographical boundaries? Crafting effective regulations requires collaboration and flexibility, ensuring that laws are as dynamic as the technology they aim to govern.

Proposed regulatory approaches offer a glimmer of hope. Risk-based regulation suggests tailoring oversight based on the potential impact of AI applications. Co-regulation, where government and industry join forces, combines the best of both worlds to ensure AI is used responsibly. This approach is akin to a buddy cop movie, where both parties work together to tackle challenges head-on.

Worldwide, regions are tackling AI regulation in unique ways. The European Union's AI Act presents a comprehensive legislative framework, setting a high bar for ethical AI use. Meanwhile, the United States offers federal guidelines that emphasize ethical considerations, such as a parent offering gentle nudges toward good behavior. These initiatives reflect diverse strategies for managing AI, each with the goal of fostering innovation while ensuring safety and fairness.

8.4 THE FUTURE OF AI: TRENDS AND PREDICTIONS

Imagine a world where computers are not just fast but mind-bogglingly quick, crunching numbers at speeds that make today's supercomputers look like snails. Enter quantum computing, the superhero of data processing. This technology, still in its infancy, holds the promise of revolutionizing AI by solving problems that currently take eons in just seconds. Picture AI systems so advanced they could predict natural disasters with incredible accuracy or crack complex medical mysteries that stump even the most seasoned doctors. But don't worry, quantum computers won't be taking over your smartphone anytime soon—they're more like the high-tech race car to our everyday sedans.

Now, hop into the driver's seat of another AI marvel: autonomous systems. These aren't just about cars driving themselves (although that's pretty cool, too). Think broader—like drones managing supply chains or robots handling logistics with the precision of a Swiss watch. Autonomous systems offer efficiency and safety, reducing human error and freeing us from mundane tasks. Imagine a world where your pizza is delivered by a drone, still steaming hot from the oven. While the technology isn't perfect yet, it's a step toward a future where logistics are as smooth as a cat's purr.

But here's where we need to pause and think. As AI grows, ethical considerations loom large. Human-AI collaboration must strike a balance between automation and human oversight. We can't have our cake and eat it, too, unless we ensure humans remain in the loop, guiding AI's decisions responsibly. Autonomous decision-making presents moral dilemmas, especially when machines make choices that affect human lives. These challenges require us to walk a tightrope between innovation and ethics, ensuring AI serves humanity's best interests.

Looking ahead, AI holds the potential to tackle global challenges. From optimizing food production to ensuring we take care of the planet, AI could be the key to unlocking solutions we've only dreamed of. It's like having a magic wand that, when used wisely, can create a better world. The possibilities are endless, and while the road ahead is full of twists and turns, one thing is certain: AI is gearing up to play a starring role in shaping our future.

8.5 UNDERSTANDING AI ETHICS: KEY ISSUES AND CONSIDERATIONS

Transparency in AI means making sure its systems aren't black boxes that spit out results without any explanation. Just like you'd want to know the ingredients in your cocktail, users should understand how AI arrives at the decisions it makes. This openness builds trust, ensuring that nobody ends up with an unpleasant surprise.

Accountability is another cornerstone of ethical AI. It's about holding AI systems and their creators responsible for their actions, like making sure the chef owns up to overcooking the roast. When AI systems make errors or biased decisions, it's crucial to identify who's liable. This kind of accountability ensures that AI developers and companies prioritize ethical standards with corrective measures in place. Without it, AI systems could cause harm without anyone to answer for them.

AI also presents ethical dilemmas that are as tricky as a game of Twister. It's vital to ensure that AI doesn't reinforce existing inequalities, which requires careful oversight and diverse training datasets. Meanwhile, AI-driven decision-making raises questions about ethics. Who decides what's right or wrong when machines make choices that affect human lives? These moral challenges demand a thoughtful approach to AI governance.

Ethical frameworks play a crucial role in guiding AI policies. By developing clear ethical guidelines, we can establish standards for AI use, providing a roadmap for responsible development and application. Regulatory bodies oversee these guidelines, ensuring compliance and fostering public trust. AI's impact on societal values is significant, too. Privacy erosion is a growing concern as AI systems collect and analyze personal data. Maintaining individual privacy in an AI-driven world is like guarding a treasure chest—challenging but essential. Additionally, AI's influence on autonomy raises questions about human independence. As AI systems take on more roles, we must ensure they complement our autonomy rather than undermine it.

8.6 AI AND PRIVACY: PROTECTING YOUR DATA IN A DIGITAL WORLD

Speaking of risks, let's discuss privacy concerns swirling around AI. With AI's power to process and analyze data, it raises questions about data security and privacy. Companies must handle personal information responsibly, ensuring data is used ethically and protected from breaches. While AI can improve security by predicting threats, it also demands constant vigilance. As users, we should remain informed about how our data is collected and used. The focus should be on creating AI systems that respect privacy, ensuring that our digital footprints don't lead to unwanted surprises.

In the realm of AI, data privacy is the guard dog, ensuring your important info doesn't end up plastered on billboards everywhere. But how do we keep this digital watchdog vigilant? Data breaches are like that one neighbor who always seems to know your business, and with AI, the stakes are even higher. Hackers are ever more cunning, and our data—from birthday wishes to shopping habits—is their treasure trove. Ensuring informed consent is crucial. People should know what data is collected and why.

The challenges in AI privacy are numerous. Data collection is like an enthusiastic squirrel gathering nuts—except these nuts are snippets of your life. The extent of personal information gathered can be staggering, and once collected, it often bounces across platforms like a hyperactive pinball. This data sharing introduces risks, as even innocuous exchanges can lead to a potential privacy nightmare.

But fret not because we have strategies to safeguard your digital secrets. Encryption is the Fort Knox of data protection, using complex algorithms to ensure your information remains as secure as a vault. Anonymization plays its part, too, removing identifiable details to protect your privacy, much like disguising your secret recipe as an ordinary cookie formula. Privacy regulations like the

GDPR and CCPA are there to keep companies in check. These frameworks act as vigilant guards, ensuring your data rights are respected and that your secret recipe remains yours and yours alone.

8.7 BALANCING AI INNOVATION WITH RESPONSIBLE USE

The drive for rapid AI innovation is like a high-stakes race, with competitive pressures pushing companies to outdo each other. It's tempting to sprint ahead, but without ethical considerations, you risk tripping over your own shoelaces. Balancing progress with responsibility requires a delicate choreography, ensuring that innovation doesn't overshadow ethical use.

Corporate responsibility plays a pivotal role in integrating ethics into AI strategies. Companies need robust AI policies, like a code of conduct for AI, ensuring ethical guidelines are established and followed. Stakeholder engagement is equally vital, involving diverse voices in AI discussions. By listening to these voices, companies can craft AI systems that reflect the needs and values of society.

Successful examples of ethical AI innovation abound. Google has established AI principles, guiding ethical development and ensuring transparency. Meanwhile, IBM's AI ethics board acts as a moral compass, steering the company toward responsible AI use. These organizations demonstrate that it's possible to balance innovation with ethical responsibility, paving the way for AI systems that serve humanity while staying true to moral values. In this ever-evolving landscape, the challenge lies in maintaining this balance, ensuring AI remains a tool for good while pushing the boundaries of what's possible.

8.8 ETHICAL AI IN PRACTICE: CASE STUDIES AND LESSONS LEARNED

Picture this: you're walking through a city where every face is recognized by cameras faster than you can say, "cheese." This is the world of facial recognition technology, where privacy concerns are as common as pigeons in the park. A notable case unfolded when San Francisco became the first major city to ban its use by law enforcement, citing privacy and surveillance fears. The move sparked a national debate, highlighting the tug-of-war between security and civil liberties. Critics argued for transparency and regulatory oversight to ensure ethical standards. Meanwhile, autonomous vehicles present their own ethical conundrums. Imagine a self-driving car faced with an unavoidable accident—should it prioritize the safety of passengers or pedestrians? These scenarios are real-world challenges that demand important ethical frameworks.

Analyzing these cases reveals vital successes and missteps. San Francisco's ban illustrates the power of public input in shaping policy, yet it also underscores the complexity of balancing innovation with privacy. The key takeaway? Ethical AI requires constant vigilance, openness to feedback, and a willingness to adapt. Public scrutiny and feedback play a crucial role in this dance. By engaging communities through consultations and transparency reports, developers can gather various perspectives, much like a potluck dinner where everyone brings a dish. This engagement fosters trust, ensuring AI technologies serve the public interest.

Ethical AI systems are more likely to gain public trust in this way through transparency. Just as you wouldn't buy a car without knowing what's under the hood, users want to understand how AI systems work. Transparency enhances communication, enabling users to make informed decisions. When AI developers prioritize ethics, public confidence increases, making it easier to incorporate AI into daily life without the fear of any unintended consequences.

8.9 ENGAGING WITH AI COMMUNITIES: ADVOCACY AND AWARENESS

In the vibrant world of AI, communities play a crucial role. Grassroots movements are driving citizen-led AI initiatives, empowering everyday folks to influence how AI impacts their lives. These platforms are vital, providing spaces for ethical discussions that reach beyond boardrooms and into living rooms. They allow all of our voices to be heard, ensuring that AI development takes shape while everyone gets to be a part of the conversation.

Advocacy organizations are the champions of ethical AI use. The AI Now Institute, for example, delves into AI's societal impact, conducting research that informs policies and practices. Meanwhile, the Partnership on AI collaborates with stakeholders to promote responsible AI development, acting as a bridge between tech companies and the public. These groups are like AI's moral compass, guiding it toward paths that respect human dignity and rights. Their work is indispensable, shedding light on the ethical implications of AI technologies and advocating for accountability in AI systems.

Raising awareness about AI ethics requires creativity and commitment. Educational campaigns are key, using engaging content to inform the public about AI's potential and pitfalls. Picture colorful infographics and catchy videos explaining AI ethics in a way that makes sense to everyone—from techies to toddlers. Workshops and seminars provide hands-on learning opportunities, equipping participants with the tools they need to navigate the ethical complexities of AI. These initiatives inspire people to think critically about AI, encouraging them to become informed advocates for responsible technology use.

Individual contributions matter, too. Volunteering in AI ethics initiatives allows you to make a difference, whether by participating in community projects or supporting advocacy campaigns. Taking an ethical AI pledge is another way to commit to responsible AI use, signaling your dedication to ethical principles. These actions, though small, collectively foster a culture of awareness and accountability where everyone plays a part in shaping AI's future. As we close this chapter, let's look ahead to how AI can be both a tool for innovation and a force for good, with individuals and communities at the heart of this transformative journey.

8.10 FINDING RELIABLE AI RESOURCES: SEPARATING WHEAT FROM CHAFF

These days, just going on an app like Facebook or Instagram can be a challenge. With all the enhancements made to generative AI, sometimes it can be difficult to spot a real video from a fake one. How do we not get tricked into falling for fake news reports, either?

With the abundance of AI resources out there, navigating your way can feel like trying to find a needle in a haystack, except the haystack is made of digital noise, and the needle might actually be a spreadsheet. The internet is brimming with AI materials, but not all of them are created equal. While sifting through this information, it's crucial to evaluate the credibility of the resources you encounter.

Next, consider the reputation of the publication. Is it a well-known journal or a reputable website? Or is it one of those sketchy sites that promises to make you a millionaire with AI in a week? Trustworthy publications tend to have a history of reliable content and are often peer-reviewed or cited by other reputable sources. This vetting process ensures that the information presented is accurate, relevant, and trustworthy. So, if you find yourself on a page that looks like it was designed in the early 2000s with flashy ads promising AI enlightenment, it might be wise to click away.

Beware of resources making overhyped claims as well, like promising to turn you into an AI guru overnight. AI is fascinating and powerful, but it's not magic. Resources that make such claims often lack depth and may gloss over important details, leaving you with more questions than answers. Additionally, ensure the content is up-to-date. AI is a rapidly evolving field, and old information can quickly become obsolete. Check the publication date and look for recent updates or revisions to ensure you're getting the latest insights.

For those looking for a solid foundation, I recommend starting with a trusted AI learning platform. Coursera and edX offer a wealth of online courses from reputable institutions like Stanford and MIT, providing structured learning paths that cater to various skill levels. These platforms are like the Ivy Leagues of online learning, offering courses designed by experts that are both informative and engaging. If you prefer reading, consider AI-focused books and academic journals. These are often penned by industry leaders and provide in-depth analyses and discussions on AI trends, technologies, and applications.

Community input plays a vital role in validating AI resources. User reviews can offer valuable insights into how effective a resource is from the perspective of fellow learners. It's like reading restaurant reviews before deciding where to eat—you get a sense of what to expect and whether it's worth your time. Similarly, expert opinions can guide you toward high-quality materials. Recommendations from AI professionals—those who live and breathe this stuff—can point you to resources that are both credible and comprehensive.

In a world overflowing with information, finding reliable resources is the key to understanding AI without getting lost in all the noise. By focusing on credibility, reputation, and community feedback, you can build a solid foundation for your AI learning adventure. This approach ensures you're well-equipped to tackle the nuances of AI with confidence and clarity. As we transition to the end of our AI for Beginners journey, remember that the quality of your sources is as important as the knowledge you gain from them.

Key Takeaways from Chapter 8:

- **Fair and ethical AI development is critical** – AI should be designed to be transparent, fair, and accountable, ensuring that it serves all individuals equally.
- **AI is revolutionizing accessibility** – AI-driven tools are empowering individuals with disabilities, improving mobility, communication, and overall quality of life.
- **AI regulation is still evolving** – Governments worldwide are working to create policies that balance innovation with ethical concerns, but regulating AI remains a moving target.
- **Reliable information on AI is essential** – With so much AI-related content online, it's important to seek trustworthy sources and stay informed about AI developments.
- **Public awareness and advocacy play a key role** – Ethical AI development benefits from community involvement, with advocacy groups and individual users contributing to responsible AI policies.

As we dive deeper into the age of artificial intelligence, it becomes clear that AI is more than just a powerful tool—it's a force that is shaping our societies, workplaces, and personal lives. With great potential comes great responsibility, and the ethical and societal implications of AI are at the heart of many critical discussions. From ensuring fairness in AI decision-making to protecting data privacy and maintaining human oversight, these considerations will define how AI is integrated into our world. The challenge isn't just about making AI smarter; it's about making sure it aligns with our values, safeguards human rights and civil liberties, and enhances—not replaces—human creativity and decision-making.

AI also plays a crucial role in creating a more inclusive world. From accessibility tools that assist people with disabilities to AI-driven mental health support and communication aids, technology is helping break down barriers that once made daily life more challenging for many. However, with these advancements comes the need for ethical oversight, ensuring that AI is used as a force for empowerment rather than exclusion. At the same time, as AI becomes more embedded in our personal and professional lives, governments and organizations are working to regulate its use—creating policies that balance innovation with public safety and ethical considerations.

Looking ahead, AI's future is filled with both promise and challenges. Striking the right balance between innovation and ethical responsibility will be crucial in ensuring that AI remains a tool that enhances society rather than disrupts it. As AI continues to evolve, the conversation around its societal impact will only grow more important. Those who understand AI's potential, its risks, and the ethical considerations involved will be better equipped to shape a future where AI is used responsibly for all.

By understanding these ethical and societal implications, we can all play a role in shaping AI's future—one that prioritizes fairness, responsibility, and ultimately, human well-being.

Bonus: A ChatGPT Prompt for Recommendations on Reputable Websites to Enhance Your AI Learning

Prompt: *"I want to continue learning about AI and how I can use it in my daily life. Can you recommend some reputable websites, online courses, or resources where I can explore AI tools, practical applications, and beginner-friendly tutorials?"*

This prompt helps users find trustworthy sources for AI education, ranging from free learning platforms to practical AI tools that can enhance their daily routines. Hopefully, throughout these chapters, these prompts have helped you become more comfortable with ChatGPT.

CONCLUSION

Well, my friend, we've reached the end of our AI adventure together! It's been quite a journey, hasn't it? We've explored the fascinating world of artificial intelligence, uncovered its mysteries, and debunked its myths along the way. From understanding the basics of AI to discovering its practical applications in our daily lives, we've covered a lot of ground in this book.

Remember when we first started, and AI seemed like this daunting, incomprehensible concept? Well, look at you now! You've learned that AI isn't just for tech geniuses in lab coats—it's for everyone, including you. We've demystified the jargon, broken down the complexities, and shown you that AI is a tool you can use to enhance your life and career with no coding skills required.

Throughout our journey, we've seen how AI is transforming industries like healthcare, finance, and education. We've explored real-world examples of AI in action, from virtual assistants to personalized learning platforms. You now have a solid grasp of how AI can streamline tasks, boost productivity, and help you make smarter decisions.

But here's the thing: your AI journey doesn't end here. In fact, it's just the beginning! I encourage you to take what you've learned and start experimenting with AI tools in your own life. Whether it's using ChatGPT to improve your writing or leveraging AI-powered apps to optimize your daily routine, embrace the power of AI and see how it can work wonders for you.

AI is a lot like a muscle; the more you use it, the stronger it gets. Just like anything new in life, it will take some time to become an expert, but AI tools like Alexa, CapCut, ChatGPT, and Fitbit have become a regular part of my day now, and it's difficult to imagine life without them. Heck, as someone used to sleeping with a fan on, there's even an app I've downloaded on my phone that plays the sound of a fan when I'm on the road!

Keep that curiosity burning. The world of AI is constantly evolving, with new breakthroughs and innovations happening every day. Stay hungry for knowledge, and never stop learning. Attend workshops, join online communities, and keep exploring the vast array of AI resources out there. The more you learn, the more you'll grow, and the better equipped you'll be to thrive in an AI-driven world.

Regular self-assessment is essential in mastering AI. This process not only boosts motivation but also deepens your engagement and learning. Experiencing the satisfaction of understanding a once daunting topic is incomparable.

You might even consider starting an AI progress journal. Record your learning milestones, challenges, and uncertainties. Such a journal acts as a tangible record of your journey, offering motivation and a clear view of your progress. It's a powerful tool to visualize how much you've learned and to keep pushing forward.

Remember, AI is not some exclusive club reserved for tech elites. It's a tool that everyone can benefit from, regardless of their background or expertise. So, don't be afraid to share your newfound knowledge with others. Be an AI ambassador, spreading the word about its potential and helping others overcome their fears and misconceptions around AI.

I want to take a moment to thank you for being such a fantastic companion on this AI adventure, and as we part ways, I would like to leave you with a final thought. AI is not here to replace us; it's here to empower us. It's a tool that can help us unlock our full potential, achieve our goals, and make a positive impact on the world. So, embrace AI with open arms, and let it be your partner in shaping a brighter, smarter future.

I'll include a list of resources here afterward, with links to AI-related apps and websites to help you further your own AI journey.

Keep exploring, keep learning, and most importantly, keep having fun! The AI revolution is just getting started, and I can't wait to see where it takes you. Remember, with AI by your side, the possibilities are endless.

Until our paths cross again, keep shining bright and making the most of this incredible journey we call life!

MAKE A DIFFERENCE WITH YOUR REVIEW

UNLOCKING THE POWER OF GENEROSITY

"At the end of the day, it's not about what you have or even what you've accomplished. It's about who you've lifted up, who you've made better. It's about what you've given back." – Denzel Washington

People who take a moment to help others—without expecting anything in return—make the world a better place. So, let's do something great together!

Would you help someone just like you—curious about AI but unsure where to start?

YOUR REVIEW COULD CHANGE SOMEONE'S AI JOURNEY

My goal with *AI Essentials for Beginners* was simple: to make learning AI easy, fun, and practical. AI is transforming the world faster than ever, and I want more people to understand it, use it, and benefit from it—whether for work, business, or everyday life.

But here's the thing—most people pick up a book because someone like **you** left a review.

A quick review helps someone else take their first step into AI. And who knows? That one step could change everything. Your review could help...

✔ A small business owner use AI to work smarter and grow faster.

✔ An entrepreneur find new ways to turn their ideas into reality.

✔ A job seeker land their dream role by understanding AI's impact on hiring.

✔ A curious learner gain confidence in an AI-driven world.

✔ An older professional not fall behind the curve when it comes to AI and technology

LEAVING A REVIEW IS SIMPLE & FREE

If this book helped you in any way, you can pay it forward by leaving a quick review. It takes less than a minute but makes a huge difference.

📍 To make a difference, simply scan the QR code below and leave a review:

https://www.amazon.com/review/review-your-purchases/?asin=B0F22TGXXW

If you love helping others, you're my kind of person. Thank you for being part of this journey!

– **Kyle Lindemann**

BIBLIOGRAPHY

Acumen Velocity. (2024). *Why cloud computing is critical for AI development.* Acumen Velocity. https://www.acumenvelocity.com/blog/why-cloud- computing-is-critical-for-ai-development

AIandYou. (n.d.). *AI basics glossary.* AIandYou. https://aiandyou.org/ai_literacy/resource_library/glossary/

Asongu, S. A., & Odhiambo, N. M. (2021). *Artificial intelligence in the industry 4.0, and its impact on poverty, innovation, infrastructure development, and the sustainable development goals: Lessons from emerging economies?* Sustainability, 13(11), 5788. https://doi.org/10.3390/su13115788

Burton, C. (2023, June 26). *The best ChatGPT prompts for employee training and development.* Thinkific. https://www.thinkific.com/blog/chatgpt-prompts-for-trainers/

Cloud Google. (n.d.). *Deep learning vs machine learning.* Cloud Google. https://cloud.google.com/discover/deep-learning-vs-machine-learning

Cook, J. (2023, July 18). *8 ChatGPT prompts to write better emails.* Forbes. https://www.forbes.com/sites/jodiecook/2023/07/18/8-chatgpt-prompts-to-write-better-emails/

Coursera Staff. (2024, July 24). *20 examples of generative AI applications across industries.* Coursera. https://www.coursera.org/articles/generative-ai-applications

DeSmith, C. (2025, February 14). *Is AI already shaking up labor market?* Harvard Gazette. https://news.harvard.edu/gazette/story/2025/02/is-ai-already-shaking-up-labor-market-a-i-artificial-intelligence/

Eloundou, T., Manning, S., Mishkin, P., & Rock, D. (2023, April). *How generative AI could disrupt creative work.* Harvard Business Review. https://hbr.org/2023/04/how-generative-ai-could-disrupt-creative-work

Encyclopaedia Britannica. (2025). *History of artificial intelligence.* Encyclopaedia Britannica. https://www.britannica.com/science/history-of-artificial-intelligence

Engler, A. (2023, June 16). *The three challenges of AI regulation.* Brookings Institution. https://www.brookings.edu/articles/the-three-challenges-of-ai-regulation/

Envoice. (2022, June 3). *How to become a senior accountant: The ultimate guide.* Envoice. https://envoice.eu/en/blog/how-to-become-a-senior-accountant-the-ultimate-guide/

Fleming, R. (2024, January 5). *The future of personal health databases.* West Tech Fest Blog. https://westtechfest.com/the-future-of-personal-health-databases/

Garbinson, M. (2024, June 7). *Exploring the impact of AI voice generator characters: Changing stories in digital realms.* DGM News. https://dgmnews.com/posts/exploring-the-impact-of-ai-voice-generator-characters-changing-stories-in-digital-realms/

Gartner. (2024, June 27). *Overcoming employee fears of AI to drive business value.* Gartner

Newsroom. https://www.gartner.com/en/newsroom/press-releases/2024-06-27-overcoming-employee-fears-of-ai-to-drive-business-value

Geeks for Geeks. (2024). *AI vs traditional programming - what's the difference?* GeeksforGeeks. https://www.geeksforgeeks.org/what-is-artificial-intelligence-ai-and-how-does-it-differ-from-traditional-programming/

Hreha, J. (2024, March 21). *19 ways to use ChatGPT to boost your productivity.* Persona. https://www.personatalent.com/productivity/ways-to-use-chatgpt-to-boost-your-productivity/

Infosys BPM. (n.d.). *AI in the banking sector: How fraud detection with AI is making banking safer.* Infosys BPM. https://www.infosysbpm.com/blogs/bpm-analytics/fraud-detection-with-ai-in-banking-sector.html

International Business Machines. (2024). *6 hard truths CEOs must face.* IBM. https://www.ibm.com/thought-leadership/institute-business-value/en-us/c-suite-study/ceo

Johnson, A. (2023, March 30). *Which jobs will AI replace? These 4 industries will be heavily impacted.* Forbes. https://www.forbes.com/sites/ariannajohnson/2023/03/30/which-jobs-will-ai-replace-these-4-industries-will-be-heavily-impacted/

Laiq, F. (2024, August 12). *Top 10 natural language processing tools and platforms.* Zilliz. https://zilliz.com/learn/top-10-natural-language-processing-tools-and-platforms

Leight, E. (2023, April 21). *AI-generated song mimicking Drake and The Weeknd pulled from streaming services.* NPR. https://www.npr.org/2023/04/21/1171032649/ai-music-heart-on-my-sleeve-drake-the-weeknd

Luansing Jr., J. (2023, May 1). *9 communities for beginners to learn about AI tools.* MakeUseOf. https://www.makeuseof.com/online-communities-to-learn-about-ai/

Lutz. (2024). *AI simplified: Understanding the basics of artificial intelligence.* Lutz. https://www.lutz.us/blog/ai-simplified-understanding-the-basics-of-artificial-intelligence

Martin, C. (2023, March 15). *Meal planning and grocery shopping with ChatGPT saved me money and time.* CNET. https://www.cnet.com/home/kitchen-and-household/meal-planning-and-grocery-shopping-with-chatgpt-saved-me-money-and-time/

Mechatronics Forum. (2025, March 10). *Artificial general intelligence (AGI): The future of AI.* Mechatronics Forum. https://www.mechatronicsforum.org/post/artificial-general-intelligence-agi-the-future-of-ai

Microsoft. (n.d.). *What are workflow automation tools and software?* Micosoft Power Automate. https://www.microsoft.com/en-us/power-platform/products/power-automate/topics/workflow-automation/workflow-automation-software-and-tools

Morgan, L. (2025, March 6). *Dispelling the myth of job displacement: AI and transformation.* InformationWeek. https://www.informationweek.com/machine-learning-ai/dispelling-the-myth-of-job-displacement-ai-and-transformation

Morgan Stanley. (2023, June 6). *How artificial intelligence could usher in a new era of productivity.* https://www.morganstanley.com/ideas/ai-in-health-care-forecast-2023

Neendoor, S. (2024, October 10). *Explore best 15 AI assessment tools for higher education.*

Hurix Digital. https://www.hurix.com/blogs/explore-best-ai-assessment-tools-for-higher-education/

N., D. (2023, June 16). *How to use ChatGPT to prepare for a job interview.* CareerHigher. https://www.careerhigher.co/career-advice/how-to-use-chatgpt-to-prepare-for-a-job-interview-134186/

Ng, A. (2019). *AI for everyone* [Online course]. DeepLearning.AI. https://www.deeplearning.ai/courses/ai-for-everyone/

Oregon State University Career Development Center. (n.d.). *AI tools for career development.* Oregon State University. https://career.oregonstate.edu/resumes-cvs-cover-letters/ai-tools-career-development

Paris, F., & Buchanan, L. (2023, April 14). *How AI is being used in everyday life: An interactive guide.* The New York Times. https://www.nytimes.com/interactive/2023/04/14/upshot/up-ai-uses.html

Rashidi, S. (2024, September 21). *How to use AI to find a job.* Forbes. https://www.forbes.com/sites/solrashidi/2024/09/21/how-to-use-ai-to-find-a-job/

Saleem, A. (2023, June 5). *Responsible AI for nonprofits: Shaping future technologies.* Data Science Dojo. https://datasciencedojo.com/blog/responsible-ai-in-non-profits/

Smith, J. (2025, March 6). *How AI is revolutionizing home renovation projects.* Lifehacker. https://lifehacker.com/home/ai-home-renovation-project

Softweb Solutions. (2024, July 30). *AI-driven adaptive learning: Personalized education strategies for students with special needs.* Softweb Solutions. https://www.softwebsolutions.com/resources/ai-driven-adaptive-learning.html

STEM Guide. (n.d.). *AI art generator: Revolutionizing the world of art!.* STEM Guide. https://stem-guide.com/ai-art-generator/

Stephan. (2023, April 3). *After recent ChatGPT ban, Italian authorities face scrutiny.* Baffic. https://baffic.com/after-recent-chatgpt-ban-italian-authorities-face-scrutiny/

Sullivan, M. (2023, October 20). *Key principles for ethical AI development.* Transcend. https://transcend.io/blog/ai-ethics

TechWinks. (n.d.). *NLP in healthcare: Improving patient outcomes with AI.* TechWinks. https://techwinks.com.in/nlp-in-healthcare-improving-patient-outcomes-with-ai/

Techy Popat. (n.d.). *Augmented reality (AR) and virtual reality (VR) in marketing: How AI is enhancing immersive experiences.* Techy Popat. https://techypopat.com/augmented-reality-ar-and-virtual-reality-vr-in-marketing-how-ai-is-enhancing-immersive-experiences/

UNESCO. (2021). *Recommendation on the ethics of artificial intelligence.* UNESCO. https://www.unesco.org/en/artificial-intelligence/recommendation-ethics

U.S. Bureau of Labor Statistics. (2025, February). *Incorporating AI impacts in BLS employment projections.* Monthly Labor Review. https://www.bls.gov/opub/mlr/2025/article/incorporating-ai-impacts-in-bls-employment-projections.htm

White, D. (2024, October 23). *AI-powered budgeting in 2024: The ultimate guide to smarter money management.* TechFunnel. https://www.techfunnel.com/fintech/benefit-ai-powered-budgeting/

Zolygin, K. (2024, December 8). *AI skills you need to master by 2025: The no-BS guide.* RushTechHub. https://rushtechhub.com/ai-skills-you-need-to-master/

GLOSSARY OF AI TERMS

- **Algorithm** – A set of step-by-step instructions that tell a computer how to complete a task, just like a recipe tells you how to bake a cake. AI algorithms analyze data and find patterns to make predictions or decisions.
- **Artificial Intelligence (AI)** – The ability of machines to perform tasks that typically require human intelligence, such as learning, problem-solving, and decision-making. Think of it as a digital assistant that keeps getting smarter over time.
- **AI-Enhanced Applicant Tracking System (ATS)** – Software used by recruiters to automatically screen resumes and rank candidates based on job requirements. If your resume lacks the right keywords, an ATS might filter you out before a human ever sees it.
- **AI-Generated Content** – Any text, image, music, or video created by artificial intelligence instead of a human. Examples include AI-written articles, deep fake videos, and AI-generated paintings.
- **AI Regulation** – Government laws and policies aimed at ensuring AI is used responsibly and doesn't cause harm to individuals or society.
- **Automation** – Using AI to perform repetitive tasks without human intervention. From chatbots answering customer questions to AI sorting your email inbox, automation helps save time and effort.
- **Augmented Reality (AR)** – Technology that overlays digital elements onto the real world, like Pokémon GO or virtual try-ons for clothes and furniture.
- **Autonomous Systems** – AI-driven machines, such as self-driving cars and delivery drones, that make independent decisions based on data, reducing human intervention in logistics and transportation.
- **Big Data & Predictive Analytics** – AI's ability to analyze massive datasets, detect trends, and predict future outcomes, used in industries like finance, healthcare, and marketing.
- **Bias in AI** – When AI makes unfair or skewed decisions due to biased training data. For example, if an AI hiring system is trained on data that favors men, it may unintentionally prefer male candidates.
- **Chatbot** – An AI-powered virtual assistant that can have conversations with people, answering questions and providing support. They're commonly found in customer service and apps like ChatGPT.
- **ChatGPT** - An AI-powered chatbot that understands and responds to text

like a human in a conversation. It can help answer questions, generate ideas, write content, summarize information, and assist with learning or work-related tasks. You interact with ChatGPT by typing a question or request (called a prompt), and it provides a response in seconds. It's like having a virtual assistant that's available 24/7 to help with writing, brainstorming, problem-solving, and more.

- **Cloud Computing** – The technology that allows AI to process huge amounts of data by storing and accessing it over the internet instead of on a personal device. Think of it like streaming movies instead of downloading them.
- **Computer Vision** – A field of AI that enables computers to "see" and interpret images or videos. It's used in facial recognition, self-driving cars, and even your phone's camera filters.
- **Conversational AI** – AI systems like ChatGPT and Google Assistant that understand and respond to natural human language, making communication with machines feel more natural.
- **Cybersecurity AI** – AI-powered security tools that detect and prevent cyber threats, such as fraud detection systems and AI-driven firewalls.
- **Data Mining** – The process of analyzing large amounts of information to find useful insights. AI uses data mining to recognize patterns and make predictions.
- **Data Visualization** – AI-powered tools like Tableau and Power BI that transform complex datasets into easy-to-understand graphs, charts, and infographics.
- **Deep Learning** – A more advanced type of machine learning that uses neural networks to process information, just like the human brain. It's what allows AI to recognize faces, translate languages, and even write music.
- **Deepfake Technology** – AI-generated videos and images that mimic real people, raising concerns about misinformation and the need for reliable content verification.
- **Digital Twin** – A virtual model of a real-world object, powered by AI. Engineers use digital twins to test machines and systems in a virtual environment before applying changes in real life.
- **Ethical AI** – The practice of ensuring AI is fair, unbiased, and transparent in its decision-making. It's about making sure AI helps people instead of harming them.
- **Explainable AI (XAI)** – AI that provides clear explanations for its decisions, helping users understand why it made a specific recommendation or prediction.

- **Facial Recognition** – A form of AI that identifies people by analyzing their facial features. It's used in security systems, smartphones, and even airport check-ins.
- **General Data Protection Regulation (GDPR)** – A major privacy law in Europe that regulates how personal data is collected, stored, and used, ensuring user consent and data security.
- **Generative AI** – A type of AI that creates new content, such as text, music, or images. Tools like ChatGPT and DALL-E use generative AI to write stories, generate artwork, and even compose music.
- **Internet of Things (IoT)** – A network of smart devices that communicate with each other using AI. Examples include smart thermostats that adjust the temperature automatically or fitness trackers that monitor your health.
- **Machine Learning (ML)** – A branch of AI that allows computers to learn from data without being explicitly programmed. Instead of following strict rules, ML models improve over time by recognizing patterns—kind of like how you get better at a video game the more you play.
- **Natural Language Processing (NLP)** – The technology that enables AI to understand and respond to human language. It's what makes chatbots, translation apps, and voice assistants like Siri and Alexa work.
- **Neural Network** – A system of AI that mimics the way human neurons connect and process information. These networks help AI "think" and make decisions by analyzing layers of data, much like how our brains learn from experience.
- **Predictive Analytics** – AI's ability to predict future trends based on past data. It's used in everything from weather forecasting to recommending the next stock to invest in.
- **Prompt** - the starting point of a conversation with AI—it's the question, instruction, or request you give to an AI system to generate a response.
- **Recommendation Algorithm** – AI systems that suggest things based on what you like. Think of Netflix recommending shows or Spotify curating playlists—it's all powered by AI analyzing your habits.
- **Reinforcement Learning** – A type of AI training where the system learns by trial and error, just like how a dog learns tricks with treats and rewards.
- **Self-Driving Car (Autonomous Vehicle)** – A vehicle that uses AI, computer vision, and sensors to drive itself without human input. Companies like Tesla and Google's Waymo are developing this technology.
- **Sentiment Analysis** – A type of NLP that determines whether a piece of text is positive, negative, or neutral. Businesses use it to analyze customer reviews and social media comments.
- **Speech Recognition** – The ability of AI to understand and convert spoken

words into text. This is how voice assistants like Google Assistant and Siri understand your commands.

- **Supervised Learning** – A type of machine learning where AI is trained using labeled data. It's like teaching a child by showing them examples first, so they can recognize patterns later.
- **Surveillance AI & Civil Liberties** – The ethical debate around AI-powered security systems that monitor public spaces, raising concerns about privacy and government oversight.
- **Sustainable AI for Climate Solutions** – AI-powered models that optimize energy consumption, predict climate trends, and improve efficiency in industries like agriculture and transportation.
- **Tech Ecosystem** – The interconnected world of technology and innovation, where AI plays a central role.
- **Turing Test** – A test created by Alan Turing to see if a machine can behave so much like a human that people can't tell the difference. If AI can pass this test, it means it has reached a high level of human-like intelligence.
- **Unsupervised Learning** – When AI figures things out on its own by analyzing raw data without labels. It's like a detective solving a mystery with only clues and no instructions.
- **Virtual Assistants** – AI-powered personal assistants like Google Assistant, Siri, and Alexa that help users with tasks such as setting reminders, answering questions, and controlling smart home devices.
- **Wearable AI Devices** – Smart gadgets like fitness trackers and smartwatches that use AI to monitor health, track physical activity, and provide real-time biometric insights.
- **Workflow Automation** – AI-powered systems that streamline business processes, such as autofilling forms, generating reports, or prioritizing emails based on urgency.

LEARNING RESOURCES TO CONTINUE YOUR AI-LEARNING JOURNEY

As you continue exploring the world of AI, there are many great resources available to deepen your understanding and build practical skills. Below is a curated list of a dozen AI-learning platforms, communities, and interactive tools, **organized alphabetically**, along with a brief description of what they specialize in and a link to access them.

1. AI and You

- **Specialty:** AI education and ethical awareness for everyday users, including underserved communities.
- **Website:** https://aiandyou.org

2. AI Dungeon

- **Specialty:** A text-based AI storytelling game that allows users to experience interactive fiction powered by AI.
- **Website:** https://play.aidungeon.io

3. AI Stack Exchange

- **Specialty:** A Q&A platform where AI enthusiasts, researchers, and developers discuss AI-related technical topics.
- **Website:** https://ai.stackexchange.com

4. Coursera (AI & Machine Learning Courses)

- **Specialty:** Online courses from top universities and organizations covering AI, machine learning, deep learning, and more.
- **Website:** https://www.coursera.org

5. DeepLearning.AI

- **Specialty:** AI and deep learning courses created by Andrew Ng, including hands-on projects and real-world AI applications.
- **Website:** https://www.deeplearning.ai

6. Elements of AI

- **Specialty:** A free beginner-friendly AI course designed to teach fundamental AI concepts in an easy-to-understand way.
- **Website:** https://www.elementsofai.com

7. IBM SkillsBuild

- **Specialty:** Free AI, cloud computing, and data science courses for learners of all levels, including certifications.
- **Website:** https://www.ibm.com/training/skillsbuild

8. Khanmigo (by Khan Academy)

- **Specialty:** AI-powered tutoring and learning assistant that helps students understand various subjects, including AI and coding.
- **Website:** https://www.khanacademy.org/khanmigo

9. Learn AI Together (on Discord)

- **Specialty:** A community-driven AI learning hub where learners, researchers, and developers collaborate and discuss AI topics.
- **Website:** https://discord.gg/learn-ai

10. r/MachineLearning (Reddit Community)

- **Specialty:** A highly active Reddit community where AI and machine learning enthusiasts share insights, research papers, and discussions.
- **Website:** https://www.reddit.com/r/MachineLearning

11. Senior Planet from AARP

- **Specialty:** AI and technology learning resources tailored specifically for seniors, helping them stay informed and engaged.
- **Website:** https://www.seniorplanet.org

12. Teachable Machine (by Google)

- **Specialty:** A beginner-friendly tool that lets users train their own machine learning models without coding.
- **Website:** https://teachablemachine.withgoogle.com

These resources provide a mix of structured courses, hands-on learning, AI-powered tools, and vibrant online communities to help you continue your AI education at your own pace. Whether you're looking for beginner-friendly courses, interactive learning tools, or advanced AI discussions, this list offers something for everyone!

LIST OF AI TOOLS MENTIONED IN THIS READING

Throughout this book, we've explored a wide range of AI-powered applications that can enhance productivity, improve health, streamline learning, and simplify daily tasks. Below is a handy reference list of all the AI-related tools mentioned, organized alphabetically. Each entry includes a brief description of what the app specializes in and a website link (if available) so you can explore them further.

- **Amazon Web Services (AWS)** – A cloud computing platform that offers AI and machine learning services for businesses and developers.
  - **Website:** https://aws.amazon.com
- **ARKit (by Apple)** – Augmented reality framework for iOS that enables AI-powered AR experiences.
  - **Website:** https://developer.apple.com/arkit
- **Arduino IoT Cloud** – A platform for building and managing IoT projects, integrating AI capabilities.
  - **Website:** https://www.arduino.cc/cloud/iot-cloud
- **Babbel** – An AI-enhanced language learning platform with interactive lessons and real-time feedback.
  - **Website:** https://www.babbel.com
- **ChatGPT** – AI-powered chatbot by OpenAI that assists with writing, brainstorming, coding, and more.
  - **Website:** https://openai.com/chatgpt
- **Cleo** – AI-powered personal finance assistant that tracks spending and provides budgeting advice.
  - **Website:** https://www.meetcleo.com
- **Cortana (by Microsoft)** – AI-powered virtual assistant that helps with scheduling, reminders, and voice commands.
  - **Website:** https://www.microsoft.com/en-us/cortana
- **DALL·E (by OpenAI)** – AI-powered image generation tool that creates original artwork from text descriptions.
  - **Website:** https://openai.com/dall-e

- **Discord** – A communication platform with AI-powered chatbots and automation for online communities.
    - **Website:** https://discord.com

Duolingo – AI-driven language learning app that adapts to users' proficiency levels for effective learning.

- **Website:** https://www.duolingo.com

- **Fitbit** – Wearable fitness tracker that uses AI to monitor heart rate, activity, and sleep patterns.
    - **Website:** https://www.fitbit.com

- **Follow My Health** – AI-powered health management app that tracks medical records and doctor appointments.
    - **Website:** https://www.followmyhealth.com

- **Google ARCore** – Augmented reality platform for Android devices, powered by AI.
    - **Website:** https://developers.google.com/ar

- **Google Assistant** – AI-powered voice assistant that helps with tasks, reminders, and smart home controls.
    - **Website:** https://assistant.google.com

- **Google Cloud IoT** – Cloud platform for managing and analyzing IoT-connected devices using AI.
    - **Website:** https://cloud.google.com/iot

- **Google Cloud Natural Language** – AI service that analyzes and understands human language in text.
    - **Website:** https://cloud.google.com/natural-language

- **Google Translate** – AI-powered language translation tool that translates text, speech, and images in real time.
    - **Website:** https://translate.google.com

- **Grammarly** – AI writing assistant that enhances grammar, clarity, and style in writing.
    - **Website:** https://www.grammarly.com

- **IBM Watson Language Translator** – AI-powered tool for translating text between multiple languages.
  - **Website:** https://www.ibm.com/watson/products-services/language-translator

- **Ideogram** – Text-to-image model designed to generate digital images from natural language descriptions, known as prompts. Unlike many other text-to-image models, Ideogram excels at producing legible text within images, making it particularly useful for creating posters, logos, and social media content.
  - **Website:** https://ideogram.ai/

- **IFTTT** – AI-powered automation tool that connects apps, services, and smart devices for seamless workflows.
  - **Website:** https://ifttt.com

- **JAWS (Job Access With Speech)** - A screen reader software designed for visually impaired users. It reads aloud on-screen text and provides keyboard shortcuts to help users navigate computers without a mouse. JAWS is widely used for accessing websites, documents, and applications, making computers more accessible for blind or low-vision individuals.
  - **Website:** https://www.freedomscientific.com/products/software/jaws/

- **Krisp AI** – AI-powered noise cancellation app that removes background noise from calls and recordings.
  - **Website:** https://krisp.ai

- **Machine Learning (Google)** – A suite of AI-powered tools for developing machine learning models.
  - **Website:** https://cloud.google.com/products/ai

- **Medisafe** – AI-powered medication reminder app that helps users track prescriptions and dosages.
  - **Website:** https://www.medisafe.com

- **Microsoft Azure AI** – AI and machine learning services offered through Microsoft's cloud platform.
  - **Website:** https://azure.microsoft.com/en-us/products/ai-services

- **Microsoft CoPilot** – AI-powered writing and productivity assistant integrated into Microsoft Office products.
    - **Website:** https://www.microsoft.com/en-us/microsoft-365/copilot
- **Midjourney** – AI-powered image generation tool that creates digital art from text prompts.
    - **Website:** https://www.midjourney.com
- **Noom** – AI-powered nutrition and weight loss app that provides personalized coaching.
    - **Website:** https://www.noom.com
- **Notion AI** – AI-enhanced productivity and note-taking tool with smart writing suggestions.
    - **Website:** https://www.notion.so
- **Pikzels** – AI-powered digital art and design tool for generating creative visuals.
    - **Website:** https://www.pikzels.com
- **Power BI (by Microsoft)** – AI-powered business analytics tool for data visualization and insights.
    - **Website:** https://powerbi.microsoft.com
- **Remodel AI** – AI-powered home renovation app that helps visualize and plan interior design changes.
    - **Website:** https://remodelai.com
- **Runway ML** – AI-powered creative tool for generating videos, animations, and graphics.
    - **Website:** https://runwayml.com
- **Strides** – AI-powered goal tracking and habit-forming app.
    - **Website:** https://www.stridesapp.com
- **Superhuman** – AI-powered email productivity tool that streamlines workflow and enhances communication.
    - **Website:** https://superhuman.com
- **Tableau** – AI-powered data visualization and business intelligence platform.
    - **Website:** https://www.tableau.com

- **Teachable Machine (by Google)** – A beginner-friendly AI tool for training custom machine learning models.
    - **Website:** https://teachablemachine.withgoogle.com

- **Trello** – AI-enhanced project management tool for organizing tasks and collaboration.
    - **Website:** https://trello.com

- **Woebot** – AI-powered chatbot that provides mental health support and emotional well-being coaching.
    - **Website:** https://woebothealth.com

- **Wysa** – AI-powered mental health app that offers emotional support and mindfulness exercises.
    - **Website:** https://www.wysa.io

- **Zapier** – AI-powered automation tool that connects different apps and workflows.
    - **Website:** https://zapier.com

www.ingramcontent.com/pod-product-compliance
Lightning Source LLC
LaVergne TN
LVHW022225200926
848481LV00006B/2128